NO WAY TO
FIGHT A
WAR

ROBERT BURNE
MacDOUGALL

COMMANDER, U.S. NAVY (Retired)

ISBN: 978-1-891029-08-0

Library of Congress Control Number: 2010920947

DISCLAIMER

This is a work of non-fiction. The information contained therein is public information. The author is responsible for the material included in this publication, with permission to use photographs, forms, resolutions, public laws, and congressional information.

About the Cover: The cover photo shows two officers assigned to Company C, 1st Battalion, 4th Infantry Regiment of the United States Army surveying the rugged mountain landscape near Forward Operation Base Lane, Zabul Province, Afganistan. The photo is a U.S. Army photo taken by Staff Sergeant Adam Mancini and is reproduced with grateful appreciation to Staff Sergeant Mancini, the Department of Defense, the Digital Video & Imagery Distribution System, and StrategyPage.com.

HENDERSON PUBLISHING

811 Eva's Walk, Pounding Mill, VA 24637

Contents

About the Author

Robert Burne MacDougall
Commander, U.S. Navy (Retired)

Robert MacDougall, a native of Westford, Massachusetts, initially enlisted in the Navy's nuclear submarine program. He was appointed to the United States Naval Academy in Annapolis by the Secretary of the Navy, where he majored in Far East Studies and Mandarin Chinese. He served a full career in the Navy, seeing extensive shipboard service as a Surface Warfare Officer and as a Special Duty Cryptologic Officer, specializing in tactical employment of signals intelligence. He holds an advanced degree from Harvard's Kennedy School of Government. Most recently, he has been an adjunct instructor at East Carolina University in the Political Science Department. Commander MacDougall and his wife currently reside in Norfolk, Virginia. Their two adult children and their spouses are all currently serving.

*This book is dedicated to
all the Soldiers, Sailors, Airmen,
Marines and their families.*

Preamble

Since the end of the Second World War the United States has entered into a costly and protracted "Cold War," four major wars and numerous smaller armed conflicts. The United States is currently contemplating expanding one of these "smaller" conflicts into a fifth major war in Afghanistan.

Unlike the Second World War these wars have lacked broad and sustained public support and public involvement. The sense of "shared sacrifice" has been lacking from the beginning or eventually lost all together.

The United States has pursued "limited wars" in remote locations without the benefit of a formal declaration of war as required by the Constitution. None of these wars have met the criteria for "limited war." Not coincidentally, none of these wars have achieved what could be called a victory. The people, the government and the military have repeatedly been frustrated by this failure to attain definitive results. The costs have been high in terms of blood and treasure and the rewards have been short-lived. An ongoing national debate over the appropriate use of armed force has split the nation along political and ideological lines unlike any other period in American history.

Following the Second World War, for the first time in its history, the United States retained a large standing military force. It retains to this day a substantial military force permanently based in foreign countries. It retains a substantial capacity for conventional expeditionary warfare in addition to its capacity for global thermonuclear warfare. In response to the retention of these capabilities and to the perceived failed effort in Viet Nam, the Congress expanded its preexisting Constitutional war powers by enacting the War Powers Resolution of 1973. The War Powers Resolution, aside from its questionable constitutionality, has led to an unhealthy politicization of national defense.

Following the tumultuous decade of the 60s the national government abandoned the military draft and created an all volunteer military force. In response to various special interest groups the government has imposed a number of social policies onto the all volunteer military that are contrary to military readiness to fight and win wars.

The combination of the aforementioned policies and practices helps to explain why the United States has failed to achieve unambiguous victory efficiently and expeditiously in every war since the end of the Second World War. Furthermore it shows why continued pursuit of these policies and practices results in a recipe for failure in the employment of military force now and in future.

Introduction

I was born in 1952. My father and several of my uncles served in various branches of the armed forces during World War II. My mother was a high school student during the war. My earliest recollections are of the stories told by the friends and families of my parents telling of the wartime and its aftermath. I was struck by how the war had impacted on the lives of everyone, young and old, men and women, boys and girls, not just the young men who served, fought and died.

My hometown, Westford, Massachusetts, is a quintessential colonial New England town. The town common, in the center of town, is flanked by two white steeple churches and is punctuated by monuments to the town's participation in the Revolutionary War, the Civil War and two world wars. The past sacrifices of the town made Memorial Day our biggest yet most solemn holiday.

Westford was essentially a farm community northwest of Boston situated approximately fifty miles from the Atlantic coast. Its principal crop was apples. While Westford had little if any strategic importance during World War II, I marveled at the impact that the war had on virtually every person in the town. Even though it was only the young men that actively participated in combat, I have always had the sense that everyone in the town at the time of the war was "vested" in the waging of the war.

The importance of this "connection" of the citizenry to the actual prosecution of a war didn't strike me until the summer of 2006. My wife and I had recently relocated from Rhode Island to North Carolina. Shortly after our arrival I was asked to teach a college course entitled "War in the Modern Age." As there was no prescribed syllabus for the course I went about "creating" the course based on what I thought an undergraduate course on this weighty subject should include.

As a retired career naval officer I had some idea where to look for fundamental reading material related to war. I wanted to provide my students with a foundation on which to build an understanding of the roughly 45 major armed conflicts currently engaged around the world.

Much to the dismay of my students, (and the university bookstore), I chose to avoid textbooks and rely instead on the writings of what

I considered "timeless" authorities on the subject of war. Aside from being timeless, I found the words of my chosen experts to be refreshingly unencumbered by the biases and political correctness permeating much of current-day literature on the subject of war. Like the affect of wasabi on the sinuses, these words awakened my mind to the true nature of war.

The source materials (all available on the Internet) I used were:

The Art of War (c. 512 B.C.) by Sun Tzu

Sun Tzu, among the first warrior/philosophers to chronicle the "truths" of war based upon personal observation and experience along with an understanding of the history of centuries of warfare within ancient China. His observations remain relevant to this day and also provide a special window into current day Chinese strategy.

Discourses on Livy (c. 1517 A.D.) by Niccolo Machiavelli

In Discourses, Machiavelli derives timeless lessons from the history of Rome as told by the official historian of Rome, Titus Livius (Livy). Livy wrote of the origins of Rome in roughly 753 B.C. and its eventual evolution into a great republic. Machiavelli, studying Livy's Roman history in the late 15th Century, had the full benefit of hindsight. In addition to benefitting from the history according to Livy, which included the height of the Roman Empire, Machiavelli was able to perceive through 20/20 hindsight, the decline and eventual dissolution of the empire into the warring city-states of Machiavelli's time.

On War (1832) by Carl von Clausewitz

Clausewitz is arguably the most important "war theoretician" in all of history. For me, his work is only enhanced by the fact that he directed that his extensive writings were not to be published until after his death. In contrast to present day writers, who are more interested in where a book falls on the New York Times or Amazon best sellers' lists, Clausewitz only cared about the content of his ideas. Of pivotal importance to this book, is Clausewitz's description of the very nature of war through what he coined as the "Trinity of War."

The Influence of Sea Power Upon History (1889) by Alfred Thayer Mahan

Mahan's work is particularly useful in gaining an understanding of sea power and its critical role in founding, achieving and maintaining the United States of America. Furthermore, Mahan provides a blunt assessment of 19th Century colonialism that helps us in understanding the roots of current-day armed conflict, particularly on the African continent.

Some Principles of Maritime Strategy (1911) by Julian Stafford Corbett

Corbett set out to finish the work of Carl von Clausewitz. Clausewitz died before completing work on the topic of limited war. Corbett defines limited war and explains how, when, and where it can exist. It is important to us today because his views shed light on what the United States and other major world powers have attempted to do since the end of the Second World War. He also gives us valuable insight into why the United States has been less than successful in bringing armed conflicts it has entered to successful and unambiguous conclusions.

On Guerilla Warfare (1937) by Mao Tse-Dung

Mao provides us with a guidebook to what is popularly called, asymmetric warfare, warfare that pits unconventional armed forces against conventional armed forces. He updates what Sun Tzu concluded more than 2500 years ago – war is reciprocal in nature. War is a series of reciprocal actions and reactions between adversaries conforming to no preordained plan or timeline.

Why I Wrote This Book

Central to the principal theme of my book is Clausewitz's "trinity theory." Clausewitz describes war as an extension of national politics that depends upon three critical elements. Much like a three-legged stool, war depends equally upon each "leg" of the trinity to be successfully waged. The first two legs are obvious, the first leg is the government the second leg is the military. The third leg, perhaps surprisingly, is the people, the citizens themselves. Historically, it is, in Clausewitz's words, the "hatreds and animosities" of the people that lead to war in the first place and it is the involvement and support of the people that are necessary to successfully prosecute, sustain and ultimately conclude a war.

Having completed my initial preparations to teach "War in the Modern Age," my wife and I escaped to Ocracoke Island, part of North Carolina's outer banks, to enjoy a weekend on the shore before beginning my class. Despite idyllic conditions on the sandy beach it was difficult for us to completely remove ourselves from events in the news. Along with my heightened state of awareness brought about by my preparations to teach, our son-in-law was about to depart on a deployment to Iraq aboard the aircraft carrier Eisenhower; our daughter-in-law was beginning flight training as a naval aviator; and, our son, a Marine Corps officer, was making preparations of his own to participate in the war.

Watching the carefree activities of the people on the beach at Ocracoke that weekend caused me to wonder – How were these people connected to the War? What "hatreds and animosities" did they hold toward our adversaries around the world? What efforts or sacrifices were these people making toward the prosecuting, sustaining and successfully concluding the current war, the Global War on Terror? If, as Clausewitz contended, the involvement of the people is essential to success in war, is it possible for the United States to be victorious in the current war or any other future war? Beyond involving the people in the prosecution of war, what can the United States do to improve its preparedness for war? What can the United States do in the future to ensure that not a drop of blood and not a penny of treasure are spent needlessly?

These questions bring me to the purpose for writing this book – Showing how, since the end of the Second World War, the United States has lost its way when determining when, where and how to wage war.

1

Robert Burne MacDougall

A Personal Journey

Clearly, "the people" are not currently engaged in the prosecuting, sustaining and concluding of armed conflicts. Except for the relatively few members of our society who are members of the "military family," the people of the United States are not connected at all to the war. As a result, without the involvement of the "People," there is very little likelihood that the United States can succeed in prosecuting, sustaining and concluding this or any future war. The likelihood of success is further diminished by the fact that our enemies know the importance of "the people" in war and it seems we have forgotten.

Having been born in 1952, part of the post war "baby boom" -

- I had a special vantage point on history following World War II. I got to appreciate the culture of my parents' generation, the "greatest generation" that fought and unambiguously won, World War II.

- I had the advantage of watching my uncles and the likes of Elvis Presley, who were not old enough to serve during World War II or Korea, continue in a tradition of service following the ceasefire in Korea and in the uncertain days of the Cold War.

- I got to participate in air raid "duck and cover" drills in elementary school. I saw empty shelves at our grocery store during the Cuban Missile Crisis.

- I avidly followed the space race from the earliest days of Project Mercury to the moon landings.

- I watched Walter Cronkite every night from the earliest days of Viet Nam.

- I watched some of my best friends get drafted and shipped off to Viet Nam while others avoided being drafted through the employment of draft deferments.

2

· I watched the tumult of the late 60s as friends participated in war protests; burned draft cards; and descended into drug experimentation and dependency.

· I voluntarily enlisted in the Navy following high school graduation and got to watch my draft number drawn, #60, a year later in a nationally televised lottery. Two years later, in my first year at the Naval Academy, I was carrying recently returned P.O.W.s on my shoulders in celebration of their recent release from North Vietnamese prisons.

· As a young shipboard naval officer, I got to suffer through the effects of the ambiguous conclusion to the Viet Nam War and the Jimmy Carter "national malaise" years.

· I experienced firsthand the waging of the Cold War at sea followed by the rush to claim the "peace dividend" following the collapse of our principle adversary, the Soviet Union.

· I have seen an Iraqi Army crushed and in retreat only to be followed by the ten-year ambiguity of "No Fly Zone" violations and "Oil for Food" corruption.

Today, there is a global struggle that threatens the very existence of the United States as a free nation, yet, our government and our news media are doing little to educate the American people as to the true nature of this struggle. Rather, the government and the news media seem to be excluding the people from the true nature of the war while selectively influencing them to achieve short-term politically motivated advantages and ends. Many within the political class seem more interested in regaining or maintaining political advantage, apparently content to accept, at best, an ambiguous outcome and, at worst, defeat.

The World War II Experience

So, what was it like on the home front during World War Two in rural Westford, Massachusetts? From anecdotal accounts from people I know

3

from other communities, I think Westford's war experience was typical of what was experienced throughout the 48 states during the course of the war.

My Uncle Jack Burne, my mother's oldest brother and eldest of seven children, was a standout high school student for most of the war. He graduated from Westford's high school, Westford Academy, in June 1944 at the age of 17. He enlisted in the Coast Guard in August of 1944, requiring parental permission from my grandfather. He came of age during the war and eventually joined the war himself in the critical final year and its immediate aftermath. My Uncle Fred Burne, child 4 of 7, was in second grade at the William E. Frost School at the time of Pearl Harbor. He became quickly and keenly aware of the war and its consequences. Based on the reflections of my uncles, Jack and Fred, I will attempt to provide a glimpse into what life was like on the home front. Their reflections provide a stark contrast between then and now in illustrating how the "people," young and old, were truly connected to the war effort.

Shared Grief

Sunday, December 7th, 1941 began as usual for the Burne family with church services in the neighboring town of Carlisle. Church began at 11, followed at noon by Sunday school. Not having a car radio, the first the family knew of the attacks on Pearl Harbor was when they returned home around 1:30. The radio waves were buzzing with the breaking news from Hawaii.

The following morning, the Frost School principal assembled the lower grade students outdoors around the school's flagpole. In simple and direct terms, the principal explained that the United States was at war with Japan. The brief and solemn pronouncement was followed by the Pledge of Allegiance to the Flag.

Soon after the initial shock of Pearl Harbor, Westford was further rattled by the news that one of Westford's own had been killed during the attack. Willard Fletcher, oldest son of a prominent farming family and brother of one of Fred's closest friends and classmate, George Fletcher, was killed aboard the Battleship Arizona. The consequences of war became even more pronounced when Willard's body was returned home for burial. All of the town's school students walked behind the funeral

4

procession en route to the cemetery. Jack, a trumpeter in the high school band, played echo taps at the ceremony. Westford and the Burne family were learning of the very real consequences of war.

Blackout Curtains and Air Raid Drills

Over the next four years the war would have an impact on virtually every aspect of daily life in our little town. Although Westford was of little strategic importance in the building war effort, the threat of air attack was nevertheless regarded as a serious matter and among the most intrusive on the lives of everyone in the town. The town was on constant alert. Frequent air raid warnings were sounded by the town's fire horns. Upon hearing the signal homes were to turn off all lights or close air raid curtains in all windows. My grandfather was the air raid warden for his street, Boston Road. Donning battle helmet and carrying a night stick, he patrolled the street looking for signs of leaking light. Not knowing whether the warning was a drill or an actual air raid, households took the alerts very seriously. Thankfully, my grandfather never used his night stick accept to occasionally rap on front doors to advise house occupants of a light leak infraction.

Air raid preparedness was not just a night-time concern. A continuous watch on the sky was kept by the townspeople. Each day was divided into four-hour "watches" in which two people, usually an adult and a teenager, would climb the ladder to the tower atop the Town Hall. For my grandfather, grandmother, and the older children of the Burne family, this meant standing a midnight to 4 a.m. watch up to three nights per week. From their high perch atop Town Hall the watchstanders could see in all directions, on a clear day or night, for a distance of roughly fifty miles. The watchstanders were equipped with aircraft identification silhouettes, a magnetic compass, and a telephone. On the rare occasion when a plane was spotted, a telephone call was placed to the regional civil defense center reporting the type of aircraft, its approximate compass heading and its compass bearing from the Town Hall.

Gas Rationing

Gasoline consumption was regulated based on need. Booklets of ration stamps, classified as "A", "B", or, "C" determined how much gasoline could be purchased per week. "A" stamps went to people who had relatively short distances to travel to work while "B" and "C" stamps permitted slightly greater amounts to permit longer commutes or operation of critical equipment like farm vehicles. My grandfather, with an "A" stamp, got 8 gallons per week. Gas allowances did not leave much room for "discretionary" driving for purposes other than going to and coming home from work places. Vacations, family outings and even going to church on Sundays had to be carefully planned and considered. It forced many to resort to mass transportation, where available, as well as to innovative driving techniques such as "coasting." Walking and bicycling were not regarded so much as forms of exercise, but rather as essential ways to get from point "A" to point "B".

The Burne family lived in a house near the center of town. The town center was situated on top of a hill. The hill afforded drivers leaving the town center the advantage of being able to shutdown or idle their automobile engines and coast down the hill. With practice, drivers could coast their automobiles for a mile or more before having to restart their engines and engage their clutches.

Guns or Butter

Another element of daily life that required careful planning involved food. Many foods, including milk, flour and butter, were rationed. Each family member was allotted a ration book with stamps. The stamps were surrendered when the food items were purchased. During the war, butter was substituted by a "lard-like substance" packaged in a pale. It was Fred's job in the household to mix into the "lard-like substance" the contents of an included packet of food coloring to make the substance appear more butter-like. As he recalls, it even tasted like butter.

Growing Up Fast

Much has been written about the fighting men of World War II being old beyond their years, of 21 year old platoon sergeants and 23 year old bomber pilots. One of the reasons was that many of these men had a running start.

As most able bodied young men went off to war, vital roles they played in everyday life fell to teenage boys. Westford, like many rural New England towns, depended, and still depend, upon volunteer fire fighters. As more and more of Westford's volunteer firemen were pressed into military service, high school boys were called upon to fill the void. The one and only perk of the job was that when the fire alarm sounded during the school day, the firefighters were permitted to bolt from class, even during exams, in order to sprint roughly a quarter mile distance from the high school to the fire house. This perk was somewhat offset by the dangers inherent with firefighting. In the case of teenage firefighters the dangers were somewhat amplified by their inexperience not only as firefighters but as drivers. A day after obtaining his driver's license, Jack Burne arrived at the station winded from the sprint from math class. The elation of escaping a test was short-lived. After a quick muster he learned that his first driving experience would not be at the wheel of the family sedan, but behind the wheel of a fire truck, laden with equipment and young fire fighters hanging on.

War Bonds, Bandages and Milk Weed Pods

As the war progressed the cost in "blood and treasure" increased. The people manning the home front were called upon to contribute in many ways. Each way, in addition to contributing to the overall war effort, perhaps most importantly, involved virtually all citizens, young and old.

School children and scout troops were enlisted in a huge war bond campaign. War bonds, purchased for $18.75, were sold door-to-door, often in school or scout-troop sponsored competitions. The bonds matured in ten years and could be redeemed for $25.

Women's groups, that during peacetime would have ordinarily met to share afternoon tea, were called into action to "wrap bandages" and package other forms of battle dressings.

Each fall, the elementary school children were encouraged to "harvest" milkweed pods from the town's open fields and pastures. The featherlike fibers inside the pods, that on other days, these same school children would delight in blowing to the wind, were collected to provide

7

the raw fibrous material used in the manufacture of floatation devises for naval and army air corps aviators' survival gear.

Shared Victory

During the war, Westford's focus was logically on the campaign in Europe. Most of Westford's small population was descended from European immigrants. The threat of air raid was from Germany, not Japan. The submarines lurking off of the Atlantic coast for much of the war were German. And the POWs "imprisoned" at nearby Fort Devins, were German. I place the word imprisoned in parentheses because of an interesting anecdote told to me by my Uncle Fred.

During the latter half of the war, Fred was employed as a newspaper boy, delivering the daily Lowell Sun. Fred's route included several streets in and around the immediate town center. The final leg of the route called for Fred to ride his bicycle back up the steep hill and into the town's center. On one fall day, as Fred was riding his bicycle up the hill on the home stretch of the route, he saw, sitting on a long roadside stonewall a large number of men brought into town to assist with the arduous task of picking apples before the first fall frost. The men were German POWs. They were casually taking in the colorful foliage and crisp fall air while awaiting transportation back to Fort Devins. Many of the German prisoners knew enough English in order to communicate with the young paperboy. For several weeks during apple picking season, the prisoners would beckon to Fred to obtain a newspaper with which they could learn of the progress of the war. The German prisoners would gather around to collectively interpret one of Fred's remaining four newspapers. They took pains to safeguard the paper for Fred so that there was no hint of it previously being used. Fred knew that his customers would take a dim view to receiving a paper that had been touched by the enemy.

Due to this close connection with the war against Germany, one would expect that the news of victory in Europe would bring about great celebration and a sense of the entire war being over, at least for Westford. This was not the case. V-E Day, May 8, 1945, came and went uneventfully. Because of the close connection between the people and the war, each man, woman and child understood that the war would not be truly final until victory over Japan. The citizens of Westford understood the "nature of war." The effects of the war had crept into virtually every facet of daily life. Each man, woman and child were, in fact, a part of the total war effort and as a result each man, woman and child were, in fact, a part of the final victory.

When, nearly four months later, on September 2, 1945, every man, woman and child shared in the joy and relief signaled by the continuous tolling of church bells – Victory!

Korea and the 50s

While I was born two years after the beginning of the Korean War and one year before the 1953 ceasefire (still in effect 55 years later), my earliest recollections are of a society still recovering from the World War II experience. Due to unresolved issues following World War II, the world divided into roughly two sides – the Free and Communist Worlds. The Korean War served as a violent demonstration of those unresolved issues and provided an initial framework for the world I grew up in and which would shape my entire 24-year military career.

Korea was fought as a "limited war." The Korean War was not even referred to as a war; rather it was euphemistically called a "police action." Unlike the recently concluded global war, the Korean War received neither a formal declaration nor a formal conclusion. Korea began a long, and yet to end, period of ambiguity in the way in which the United States goes to war.

World War II and Korea shaped my early life. My parents, my grandparents, my uncles and aunts, my parents' friends, all had lasting and vivid memories of the war experience. I was fascinated by the stories about what life was like on the home front during the War, stories of blackouts, air raid warnings and gas rationing. My curiosity was peaked even more by what was not said. None of the gatherings of friends or family ever seemed to include stories about what I was really interested in – the War itself. No one that actually participated in combat was talking.

9

Our next door neighbors, Peggy and Fred Steinman, were frequent visitors at our house. Having no children of her own, Peggy considered me to be "her baby." Even after they moved away, Peggy and Fred paid annual visits at Christmastime. My brother, sister and I looked forward to receiving their "signature gift," a new book, each year. By the age of around four I had attended many gatherings of friends and family and had heard many stories of the war years. I had come to conclude that all men of my father's age group had served in the military during the war. Out of innocent curiosity I began asking the men in my father's circle of contemporaries what they had done during the War. None of them, Fred Steinman included, ever gave me a straight answer. Fred, as I recall, simply confirmed that he had indeed served during the war. The mystery only heightened my curiosity. I was to later learn from my father that Fred was an Army veteran and survivor of the first wave of the Normandy invasion at Omaha Beach.

The euphoria brought about by the World War II victory was short-lived. As I became increasingly aware of what was going on around me so too seemed to be the public awareness of the growing threat of global thermonuclear war. By the mid to late 50s I became aware of the continued military draft. Uncles and neighbors were drafted into military service. My parents, grandparents and aunts and uncles seemed to be taking military service in stride, as a patriotic duty and tradition. In 1958, the year I entered first grade, I remember the big hubbub created when a popular performer of the time, Elvis Presley, was drafted. The news coverage of Elvis having a physical, Elvis swearing in, Elvis getting a haircut, was inescapable. The Elvis drafting, while tumultuous from a popular culture standpoint, also seemed to provide a calming reassurance that the draft was fair and impartial.

Around the time of the Elvis hysteria I also became aware of the importance of baseball in the American culture. To the dismay of my father, around 1957 I became particularly interested in the accomplishments of Mickey Mantle of the New York Yankees. I showed little interest in my father's hero, Ted Williams, of the Boston Red Sox. With each passing year; however, I became more appreciative of Ted Williams and my heritage as a "long suffering" Red Sox fan. With my already well established interest in military history, I came to appreciate Ted Williams, not so much for his baseball talent but for the fact that he was a reserve officer and combat pilot in the Marine Corps. I learned of his sacrificing critical years of his career due to World War II and the Korean War. I was even more impressed when I read accounts of his combat missions over Korea. For me, Ted Williams' sacrifice and military service reinforced the service ethic already ingrained in me by my extended family and neighbors. While I was not necessarily determined to seek a military career, I knew that my life would be less than complete without at least serving in the military for a period of my life.

While the United States was not in an active "shooting war" during the latter part of the 1950s, preparedness for war was on the minds of everyone. Even in the small farm town of Westford, we were surrounded by daily reminders of the menacing and growing Cold War. Most of the infrastructure that was erected during the Second World War remained active. We frequently saw long convoys made up of jeeps and 2 ½ ton trucks from nearby Fort Devins. Frequently we heard the distant booming of artillery from the fort. Daily I would race outside to watch a growing variety of tactical military aircraft that flew from Hanscom Field in Bedford. The sonic booms of supersonic airplanes were practically a daily occurrence. One of our neighbors, Air Force Colonel "Chip" Collins, was a famous Air Force test pilot. Colonel Collins liked to fly over our farm while testing out navigation equipment aboard a red and white specially configured helicopter. Once or twice we marveled at the sight of huge Navy blimps, slowly and quietly floating by. The blimps were stationed out of South Weymouth, a naval air station south of Boston. Even more impressive were the B-52s regularly flying out of Westover Air Force Base in Chicopee, Massachusetts.

The dawning "nuclear age" was major news in New England. The first nuclear submarines were built in Groton, Connecticut. The Portsmouth Naval Shipyard, in Kittery, Maine was prominent in the maintenance and repair of the new subs that could submerge for indefinite periods of time limited only by how much food could be stored aboard for feeding the crews. Beginning with the launching of USS Nautilus in January of 1954 from her builder's yard on the Thames River in Groton, Connecticut, the exploits of nuclear submarines was big news throughout New England and the world. With the submerged crossing of the

North Pole during the summer of 1958, Nautilus captured the imaginations of school children with the many possibilities presented by the use of nuclear power.

In answer to the threat of the Soviet Union's long-range bomber fleet, a system of Nike anti-aircraft guided missile sites were constructed throughout the country. New England was then home to many military facilities. The Boston area was a major "player" in what President Eisenhower referred to as the "military-industrial complex." Consequently, Nike missiles became a common part of the local landscape for a brief period until the long range bombers were supplanted by ICBMs stored in underground silos within the Soviet Union.

A month after I began first grade, my classmates and I at William E. Frost School, were captivated by another element of the Cold War – the space race and Project Mercury. The following spring, we joined in the frenzy of excitement and anticipation that accompanied the announcement of the Mercury Seven Astronauts. For the next several years, we would follow the space program in Weekly Reader, National Geographic, Life Magazine, and on our black and while televisions. Space exploration became the symbolic clash of good versus evil; East versus West; communism versus democracy. Like World War II was for our parents, the manned space program was a unifying endeavor that seemingly united the country in a noble cause. In many respects the Mercury Seven Astronauts, made up of brave military test pilots, some of whom had flown in combat, seemed to provide a bridge between the World War II generation and those of us now known as Baby Boomers.

The 60s and Viet Nam

The early 1960s didn't "feel" any different than the late 1950s, at least for the first five years or so. In addition to the space program, our imaginations were now captivated by the presidential election of 1960. I am not sure exactly what caused it, perhaps the fact the John Kennedy was from Massachusetts and a Catholic, but my third grade class divided itself along political and religious lines. We discovered that during the great "school recess" debates of 1960 that Catholics were Democrats and they favored Chevrolets, while Protestants were Republicans that favored Fords.

Regardless of our religious and political leanings, virtually all of my classmates and I were excited by the promise for the future outlined in President Kennedy's Inaugural Address. His exhortation to "ask not what your country can do for you - ask what you can do for your country," seemed to provide a natural "passing of the torch," a challenge, from the generations of the First and Second World Wars to my generation.

The early 60s was a period of not only hope but also nervous anticipation. My third-grader oversimplification seemed to be confirmed by the statements made by President Kennedy in his Inaugural Address and in statements made early in his administration. It appeared that the world was divided in black and white terms. Communism was expanding and threatening to make good on Nikita Khrushchev's threat – "we will bury you," made four short years earlier. The Soviet Union, which had incorporated most of Eastern Europe following the Second World War, now, included communist North Korea and China within its sphere of influence. Most threatening for the United States, the Soviet Union was increasingly expanding its influence in the Western Hemisphere. Cuba, which had fallen to communist revolutionaries led by Fidel Castro in 1958, was increasingly cozy with the Soviets. Communist expansion threatened to spread to countries in South East Asia, South America and parts of Africa.

My friends and I tended to be interested in sports, principally baseball, and "playing" army. Following Ted Williams' retirement at the end of the 1960 season, the Red Sox became even more irrelevant. The Yankees with the likes of Mickey Mantle, Roger Maris and Whitey Ford were the team to follow. It would not be until several years later that the Red Sox, led by Ted Williams' "heir," Carl Yastrzemski, would recapture forever the hearts of most New Englanders. As for playing army, my friends and I were captivated by the recent history of World War II, of Korea, and now of the Cold War that was now threatening to plunge the world into nuclear war.

Our interests were largely fed by the toy industry, the entertainment industry, and the continued dominance of war, or impending war, in the conversations of our parents. My friends and I saved our meager allowances in order to purchase scale styrene plastic models of combat

13

aircraft, ships and vehicles. When the snow-shoveling and lawn-mowing money ran out, my best friend Kevin Blanchard and I resorted to building miniature models made of cardboard and toothpicks held together with Elmer's Glue. For the more affluent among us, 1963 was the "birth year" of G.I. Joe. This was the first "action figure" that could be attired in different military uniform combinations. Besides being beyond my budget, G.I. Joe struck me as a "Barbie Doll" for boys. It never really caught on with me or any of my close friends.

In addition to the small scale toys and creations the toy industry provided us with "weapons." For not too much money one could outfit oneself with a field jacket and canteen from an army surplus store that we could adorn with iron-on or sew-on patch insignia for various infantry units. Rank insignia could usually be found by rummaging through attic storage trunks containing the war uniforms of our fathers and uncles. Replica firearms ranging from hand grenades to Thompson submachine guns were readily available at the local toy store. Ammo, reels of black powder "caps" were usually available at the local general store. The caps gave our plastic rifles, pistols and submachine guns the sound, smoke and "aroma" of battle that we wished to recreate. The one thing we had difficulty finding was battle helmets. None of the army surplus stores had the steel helmets that we needed to complete our "ensembles." Some of us resorted to constructing helmets out of papier-mâché.

Luckily for boys of my generation, our burning curiosity about the things our fathers and their contemporaries refused to tell us about was somewhat relieved by the entertainment industry of the day. The early 60s was the heyday for war-related entertainment; a period which depicted war as something both noble and exciting.

The first movie I ever went to see was at the Chelmsford Drive-in Theater. The movie was the 1962 epic, *The Longest Day*. The first movie I saw in an indoor theater was *The Bridge on the River Kwai*. *Bridge* was the Best Picture of 1957 and it made a return to theaters in the early 60s. During the summer of 1963 my friends and I piled into the back of a station-wagon to watch PT-109 at the Gloucester Drive-in. The list of movie-theater offerings were augmented by television. 1962 was a banner season with the premiere of *Combat* and *McHale's Navy*. *Combat* followed the exploits of an Army infantry platoon fighting its way across

France during World War II. *McHale's Navy*, while entertaining, was a bit silly for those of us looking for the true nature of the war of our fathers'. Most of us watched it for the fleeting moments showing the PT boats speeding through the waters of the South Pacific. A couple of years later the aviation fanatics among us were happy to see the television version of the great 1949 movie, *Twelve O'clock High.*

Our childhood world of make believe was interrupted during the fall of 1962 by something very real and very serious, the Cuban Missile Crisis. While it would be many years before we would learn the full extent of the crisis, nevertheless, this crisis got everyone's attention. Aside from the increased awareness of proper "radioactive fallout" procedures, probably the most telling sign of widespread fear was found at the grocery stores. In New England a common occurrence prior to snow storms and hurricanes is a run on store shelves for staples such as milk and bread. During the Cuban Missile Crisis the run was on everything, especially canned goods. Grocery store shelves normally loaded high with canned soups, beans and sardines were cleared. For a fifth grader it provided stark evidence that the adults regarded this crisis as real and immediate. Canned goods were being horded in expectation of needing to survive an extended period of time hunkered down in the basements of our homes in makeshift fallout shelters.

The Cuban Missile Crisis brought home to all of us how serious the Cold War was and how, unlike in all the wars since the Civil War, this war had the potential to impact directly as well as indirectly on each of us. During the early 60s, the Cold War provided a backdrop or undercurrent to virtually every aspect of daily life. Even the interstate highway system that began bisecting Westford at this time was also part of the changes in our daily lives caused by the Cold War. The interstate system, devised during the Eisenhower years, was all part of a national defense strategy. Interstate Route 495 was part of a system created by the National Interstate and Defense Highways Act of 1956.

For an elementary school student the early 60s provided a curious blend of fear, excitement, anticipation, innocence and hope. In retrospect I guess these mixed emotions were brought about by the Kennedy presidency superimposed on the Cold War. This all changed on November 22nd 1963. Unlike December 7th 1941, a day that, while living in infamy, helped to define a generation and bring out the best in the American people, November 22ⁿᵈ 1963 would provide a watershed that, while helping to define my generation, did not provide the impetus to achieve greatness or overcome evil. If anything, the assassination of President Kennedy marked the beginning of a slow decline in our national will from which we have not yet recovered.

The presidential election of 1964 was the second presidential campaign that I have any recollection of. It was made memorable for me by two things. First, my father was actively involved in the campaign for Barry Goldwater. I can trace my lifelong interest and passion for politics and world events to my father's example. The second thing was the "Daisy" television advertisement. The ad depicted a little girl counting daisy petals. Her voice is replaced by a man's voice counting down to the launch of a missile. The camera zooms in on one of the little girl's eye pupils to show the reflection of a nuclear mushroom cloud. President Johnson's voice tells the viewer that "these are the stakes, we must love one another, or, we must die." The viewer is exhorted to vote for President Johnson.

For me, the campaign of 1964 and the "Daisy" ad, turned the societal fissure, created by President Kennedy's assassination, into a gaping crevasse. It marked the beginning of a period in our history where the people were intentionally divided for political purposes; a period, yet to end, in which many politicians placed the acquisition and holding of political power above national unity and universal national interests.

During the Kennedy years, the United States continued to push back against the expansion of communism around the world. In Southeast Asia the United States was providing a growing cadre of military advisors to assist South Viet Nam in resisting a communist encroachment from the North. Like the still simmering Korea, Viet Nam was regarded as a surrogate war pitting democracy against the communism of the Soviet Union and the Peoples' Republic of China. Between 1961 and the time of President Kennedy's assassination the cadre of advisors had grown from roughly 600 to approximately 16,000.

The summer of 1964 was not only heated up by the political campaign between President Johnson and Senator Barry Goldwater. Between August 2ⁿᵈ and August 4ᵗʰ two United States Navy ships, *USS Maddox* and *USS Turner Joy*, operating in international waters in the South China Sea, apparently came under fire from naval vessels of North Viet Nam. These attacks came to be known as the Gulf of Tonkin Incident. President Johnson declared this incident to be an "unprovoked" attack. Within less than a week Congress passed what became known as the Tonkin Gulf Resolution. The Resolution provided President Johnson congressional authority to provide military assistance to South Viet Nam. The Resolution is significant because it reinforced the precedent set during the Korean hostilities – authority to go to war without a formal declaration of war.

The Resolution was passed in both houses of Congress with overwhelming majorities. In the Senate the vote was 88-2 in favor, and in the House of Representatives it was unanimously affirmed by a vote of 414-0.

The Tonkin Gulf Incident resulted in direct counter attacks on forces of North Viet Nam and with the Tonkin Gulf Resolution in hand, led to a rapid escalation of the war. For the remainder of 1964, through 1965 and into 1966 the Viet Nam War, while not necessarily popular, was regarded as a justified war by most of the people I was influenced by during my junior high school years. I recall reading about, how; unlike during World War II, Americans would not have to choose between "guns or butter." We would be able to afford the expense of fighting a distant war without having it impact on our daily lives. For the most part, my classmates seemed oblivious to the growing involvement and the growing number of deaths and casualties of the war. We had "guns and butter."

During 1964 my interest in the military services continued to grow, although it had become seemingly less "main stream" than it had been just a year earlier. Luckily, a new classmate, Stephen Gillies, had recently moved to town. Stephen's father worked for AVCO, the company responsible for manufacturing the heat shield for the Apollo spacecraft. Stephen was interested in aviation and we avidly followed the major developments in the space program and military aviation through our subscriptions to *Air Progress* magazine. By 8th Grade, Stephen and I were poring over college catalogs to the service academies. Stephen intended to apply to the Air Force Academy in Colorado Springs and I was determined to one day apply to the Naval Academy in Annapolis.

In early 1964 began a string of cultural events of major proportions that would ultimately further divide a country already splitting along political lines by the presidential campaign. It began with the arrival of the Beatles in February. My first indication that things were about to change was during the regular Wednesday afternoon practice of our church's junior choir. One of the girls was listening to WBZ AM Radio out of Boston through a single earphone attached to a transistor radio hidden in her clothes. We were in the middle of practicing the hymn *Let There be Peace on Earth* when she gave out a blood-curdling scream. The choir would soon learn *I Want to Hold Your Hand* was playing at the time.

The Beatle's February performance on the Ed Sullivan Show was the beginning of what became known as the "British Invasion." The music and the appearance of the British invaders was a marked difference from the music and appearance of our parents' generation. The music and appearance changes captivated my generation. As the 60s progressed the behavior of the "invaders" also took hold with a majority of my contemporaries in high school; those of us who still got haircuts and remained transfixed by the space race, were socially "left in the dust." In addition to the normal changes of adolescence, my world was flooded with a series of parallel events and cultural changes. I watched in stunned bewilderment as one friend after another succumbed to the temptations of the age. The neat social order of my earlier childhood was being torn to pieces.

Between 1964 and 1966 the several competing and ongoing events served to further divide the country. The Civil Rights movement and President Johnson's "Great Society" were in full swing. Even for someone who tended to favor the more conservative leanings of his parents, the words of Martin Luther King Jr. and the good intentions of the Great Society were appealing. The space program was progressing with confidence and purpose toward the ultimate goal, set by President Kennedy on May 25th 1961, "before this decade is out, of landing a man on the moon and returning him safely to earth."

Shortly after President Johnson's inauguration in January 1965, the Viet Cong attacked American military advisors at Pleiku in South

Viet Nam. In response to this attack what was to be a three-year air campaign against North Viet Nam began. Along with the air assault by Navy and Air Force aircraft came a rapid build-up of American ground forces in South Viet Nam. With the increased numbers came increased casualties on the ground and the loss or capture of aviators prosecuting the air campaign in the North.

During these years I began a habit of watching the nightly news while I ate my supper. Almost every evening I would ask my mother if she would mind if I skipped supper at the family dinner table so that I could get the latest news from the War. The half-hour news with Walter Cronkite was usually a summary of war casualties and what came to be known as the "body count" of enemy killed. With improvements in video processing it became possible to see audio-video reports of combat action in Viet Nam soon after the events occurred.

The coverage of the War evolved over time. At first the coverage in both print and electronic media seemed to be focused on the skill and bravery of our armed forces under very trying conditions. I distinctly remember reading Time Magazine cover stories about Air Force pilots. Slowly, cheerleading evolved to skepticism and finally to open cynicism. In retrospect, like the "chicken or the egg," I am not sure which came first, a cynical media, a cynical Congress, or, a cynical public. Whatever the case, the end result was a case of one "feeding off" the cynicism of the other two. Unfortunately, I watched as the object of the collective scorn became the American military.

In early 1966 the Senate attempted to carry out an option afforded by the Tonkin Gulf Resolution – the repeal of the very resolution that "authorized" military action in the first place. Although unsuccessful, this action opened the door for greater and greater questioning of the War and its continued funding. In effect, Congress by not "declaring" war in accordance with its war powers enumerated in the Constitution had provided itself an "escape clause" or "trap door" by which to quickly extricate itself from the "unpleasantries" of a difficult war. By its actions Congress began giving new meaning to the phrase: *When the going gets tough, the tough get going.* The lack of resolve on the part of the Congress further fed the growing frenzy of discontent among draft eligible young men and their willing partners in the media.

19

The Democrat Party had controlled the Executive branch and both houses of Congress since President Kennedy's inauguration in 1961; therefore, it was of major importance to the national debate on Viet Nam when in October 1967, future House Speaker, Thomas "Tip" O'Neill, broke publicly with President Johnson and opposed continuation of the Viet Nam War. By early 1968 unity within the Democrat Party and support for the War seemed to come unglued. The January Tet Offensive was wrongly portrayed by the media as a major defeat of American ground forces. The My Lai Massacre of March became emblematic of the quality and character of the military in general – Soldier = Baby Killer. By the end of March President Johnson announced to a national television audience that he would not seek reelection.

By the end of 1968 draftees accounted for 38 percent of the troops in Viet Nam. For those of us at or nearing draft age, discontent with the War was "all about the draft." A complex array of "draft deferments" along with perceived, and real, political influence over local draft boards, resulted in what was regarded as, at worst, corrupt, at least, inequitable administration of the selective service system. A confluence of events and national movements resulted in a system that was looked upon by those of draft age as one that favored the affluent and well educated and punished the less affluent and less educated.

The Presidential Election of 1968 was famous for the candidate that didn't even get the nomination – Eugene McCarthy. Senator McCarthy did not even win the New Hampshire Primary on the 12th of March. He succeeded in running as an anti-war candidate that did well enough in New Hampshire to rattle President Johnson. McCarthy's appeal to voters solely on an anti-war theme emboldened Robert Kennedy to announce his candidacy for president on March 18th, as an anti-war candidate. Robert Kennedy had previously established himself as an early opponent to the War when he resigned as President Johnson's Attorney General in September 1964. Kennedy had then gone on to be elected as a U.S. Senator for New York less than two months later. President Johnson further contributed to the war related turmoil of that month when, on the evening of March 31st, in a television broadcast address to the nation he stated: "I shall not seek, and will not accept the nomination of my party for another term as your president."

In short order the 1968 election became a referendum on the Viet Nam War. The California Primary in early June became a showdown between the anti-war candidates, Eugene McCarthy and Robert Kennedy. Kennedy, as the "next in line to the throne" of the Kennedy "political dynasty" and as the younger and more charismatic of the two anti-war candidates, quickly became the one most likely to succeed in winning his party's nomination. Kennedy narrowly defeated McCarthy in the crucial June 4th primary gaining 46 percent to McCarthy's 42 percent. Tragically, immediately following his victory speech in the ballroom of the Ambassador Hotel in Los Angeles, Kennedy fell to the assassin's bullets of Sirhan Sirhan. Kennedy's death came as a major blow to not only the nation but also the growing anti-war movement. His young supporters, already roiled by the progress of the war and the inequities of the draft were further disenfranchised by this sudden turn of events. The nation, still in shock from the assassination, two short months earlier, of Martin Luther King Jr., appeared to be in danger of coming "unglued."

Kennedy's death left Senator McCarthy as the candidate of the anti-war movement, largely comprised of young people, many of whom were draft eligible males not yet eligible to vote. Following President Johnson's withdrawal from the race, his vice president, former Senator Hubert Horatio Humphrey of Minnesota, announced his candidacy. Due to the late date of his entry into the campaign, Vice President Humphrey was not eligible for any of the remaining presidential primaries. By the time of the Democrat Party's national convention in late August, the two principle candidates were McCarthy, the anti-war/anti-establishment candidate, and Humphrey, the civil rights/labor/establishment candidate. McCarthy was viewed by his supporters as the only legitimate candidate because of his participation in the primary process. They viewed Humphrey as not only an illegitimate candidate but also as the candidate who would likely follow the policies of President Johnson. Since the anti-war movement believed they had defeated President Johnson and his policies earlier in the year, the mood was ripe for conflict at the Chicago convention of late August.

In one short year we had gone from the "summer of love" to a summer of hate and discontent. As I prepared to enter my junior year in high school I was immersed in a simmering "soup" of conflict. Over the last year, while not expressing a majority view, the anti war sentiment had boiled over into open violence as protests, especially on college campuses heightened. Of course this "soup" of conflict was further complicated by the continued rise in popularity of psychedelic drugs and alcohol use among teen-agers and college students. Acid rock, music that had peaked in popularity in 1967, coupled with the rise of radical feminism, continued racial conflict, and now with a full-blown anti-war movement, set the stage for a very confusing time for me as I was trying to decide what I wanted to do with my life after high school graduation. Now was the time for me, in the college preparatory track of public education, to decide where I wanted to continue my education. The prospect of attending a large state college, like my older sister, Cynthia, then at the University of Massachusetts in Amherst, was horrifying.

To make matters worse, things got so bad during the summer of 1968 and leading up to the November election, the main issue shifted from the War to "law and order." Even though Richard Nixon promised to end the War he recognized that the people that were going to elect him were more concerned about domestic tranquility than they were about a distant war that affected them little. Despite the strong third-party challenge put on by George Wallace of Alabama, Nixon won the election handily. Of course the apparent dismissal of the War as the central issue of the election further enraged the college students and draft conscious teenagers. The anti-war movement continued to grow over the last two years of high school. Increasingly, politics and war crept into the classroom. It was not uncommon to hear a biology teacher or a typing teacher talk about the "injustice" of the War.

Other than the occasional "off topic" classroom lectures on the evils of the war and the nightly news, there was little to remind us that we were a nation at war. On the day we learned that a recent graduate of our high school had been killed in action in Viet Nam, I recall it being talked about in hushed terms. Since it was predominantly non-college prep students that were drafted into the Army there was rarely a personal connection between those of us in the "majority" college prep program and those recent grads being drafted and actively serving in the Army. Usually someone would pull a copy of the recently deceased serviceman's yearbook off the shelf in the school library; lookup the serviceman's picture in the "graduate pages" in order to connect a face to the name. We would silently nod our heads as we recognized the deceased as someone we remembered seeing in study hall or during lunch period, the only two times during the day when "college prep" intermingled with "votech". That was it. No school memorial assemblies. No funeral processions through the center of town. Long gone were the days when everyone in the town felt "connected" to the deceased or when school children marched to the burial ceremony as they had for Willard Fletcher shortly after Pearl Harbor.

Over the last two years in high school I became increasingly disconnected from my classmates. It was not just because I was a painfully shy nerd; a lonely long distance runner on the track team; a member of the weather club; the yearbook photographer who observed school activities from behind the lens of a camera; it was because I felt more kinship with an earlier generation than with my own. While my classmates revered "townies" who attended Woodstock in August of 1969, I revered the Apollo astronauts and the few friends I knew serving in the military. My last year of high school was punctuated by the nearly tragic Apollo 13 mission in April 1970, and, a month before graduation, a real tragedy at Kent State University on May 4th.

My high school academic performance had been "adequate" to graduate but not nearly good enough to even consider applying to my "first choice," the Naval Academy in Annapolis. Even though I applied, my record of achievement and SAT scores were not good enough to gain admission to my second choice, the Coast Guard Academy. While I probably could have gained admittance to a state university, my heart was not in it. I just could not see myself immersing myself in the campus-life dominated by drug experimentation, "free love," and war protest demonstrations. Knowing that the course I was on would forfeit the "holy grail" of college education at the time, a college draft deferment, I began the process of figuring out how to control my own destiny.

I began my research by collecting every military recruitment brochure from the racks at the Westford post office. It did not take me long to realize that my calling was to become an Army helicopter pilot, one of the brave young pilots who would deliver troops into combat or transport the wounded to field hospitals. With my ambitions in hand, I drove to our nearest big city with a recruiting station, Lowell. The various service recruiters were all housed in an imposing granite structure in the center of the city. Upon entering I went directly to the Army recruiter's office and told the sergeant behind the desk that I wanted to be a helicopter pilot. The sergeant's jaw dropped in disbelief that someone was actually volunteering to become an almost certain casualty of war. While dumbfounded, the sergeant composed himself and told me he would not even talk to me about the warrant officer aviation program until after I had taken "the test," a basic multiple choice aptitude test given to all potential military recruits.

My initial reaction was shock. Didn't this recruiter know what an inconvenience it was to drive all the way to the city; find a parking space in a pay lot; and, then walk several city blocks to the recruiting station? Couldn't he at least answer some questions? After timidly thanking the sergeant for his valuable time I figured since I was already there and I had to pay for a full hour of parking anyway, I might as well pick-up literature at the other recruiters - Marines, Air Force, Coast Guard and Navy. Each recruiter had about the same approach. "Take the test, and then we'll talk to you." That is until I reached the Navy office. The Navy recruiter invited me into his office and he engaged me in a conversation, before he mentioned anything about taking a test. After explaining that I was intending to become a helicopter pilot in the Army the Navy recruiter began explaining the nuclear power program, specifically nuclear submarines. Having "sized me up" he felt that the submarine program was best suited for my academic background and serious personal demeanor. Little did I know at that moment, but I had found my "home" for the next twenty-five years of my life.

For the next several months I underwent various tests and physical exams in order to fully qualify for the nuclear submarine program. Ironically, the test that the Army recruiter had insisted I take before entering into any discussions, I did very well on, well enough to qualify for the helicopter pilot program, and all other programs that the Army had to offer at the time. After taking a more advanced pre-test, a new Navy recruiter I was working with informed me that I had not only done well enough to qualify for the nuclear program, I had also done well enough to be considered for application to the Naval Academy in Annapolis. He said I should remember that in case I decided I wanted to go to college. I just had to decide before I was 22.

By the time graduation night in June of 1970 came, my mind was on "adventures at sea" not on the words of our class song, *Aquarius*, from the rock musical - *Hair*. I had hated school. I could not wait to get on with my life, somewhere other than my little ancestral hometown of Westford.

Over the next few months I prepared myself physically and mentally for the coming "rigors" of boot camp. As one of the perks of the nuclear power program, I got to choose where I wanted to attend boot camp. At the time, the Navy had three boot camps, one in Great Lakes, Illinois, one in San Diego, and one in Orlando. As it appeared that I would be attending boot camp in the late fall or early winter, I thought Orlando sounded good, certainly better than the frigid shores of Lake Michigan. The parting words from my recruiter were: "You're lucky; they'll let you come home for Christmas."

On the morning of November 19th, 1970 my parents drove me to Boston where I was "sworn-in" at the Fargo Building on Summer Street in Boston's south side. From there I took the short drive to Logan Airport to embark on my first airliner trip. My "adventure" had begun.

Welcome to the Navy

Upon arrival at the airport in Orlando, I and several hundred other new recruits were shuttled to the Recruit Training Center by battleship grey school buses. Before even leaving the airport, we were introduced to "Navy language" consisting mainly of the liberal use of human reproductive acts and sexual organs taking the new and novel forms of nouns, verbs, adjectives and adverbs. We were all separated into "companies" consisting of 80 men. My company was #202, led by a Machinist Mate Chief Petty Officer with the last name of Clark. (For the duration of boot camp since we referred to Chief Clark as "sir" we never achieved first name familiarity). One company, not mine, was made up completely of college graduates, a glaring example of the effect of the draft. My company was made up of a hodgepodge of mostly teenagers, mainly from Texas, New Mexico, Mississippi and Alabama. As a naïve 18 year old from Massachusetts, I was definitely in the minority. The most common phrase at boot camp among recruits was: "Where you from?" We were all homesick. In my company it was varied slightly to: "What part of Texas you from?" I eventually learned to reply that Massachusetts was in northeast Texas.

I also learned that our company and all the other companies formed on that day would not be going home for the holidays. We would just be completing the "primary" (most unpleasant) phase of training prior to Christmas. We surmised that we were too much of a "flight risk" if we were allowed to leave recruit training at that point. If the knowledge that our recruiters had "lied" to us was not bad enough, we got the word that we would be entering the dreaded "service-week" over the holidays. Service-week was a one week period that separated the six-week "primary" phase of training from the six-week "advanced" phase of recruit training. During service-week recruits were assigned to various labor-intensive jobs that supported the day to day operations of boot camp. Most of us were assigned to "mess cooking," a generic term assigned to all phases of food services. It involved getting up at 3 a.m. and working until nearly midnight. My particular area of responsibility was monitoring and maintaining the butter patty dispenser as well as the milk dispensers. I also learned how to make Thousand Islands salad dressing by the gallon. Of course after each meal we had to move all tables and chairs in the dining hall so that we could wash and wax the deck (Navy word for floor). We all became (floor) "buffer techs" during this period. On Christmas Day the powers that be were "compassionate" enough to allow us to stop by the telephone exchange to make a ten-minute call home. For most of us "the call" did not go well. Virtually all of us ended up "blubbering" like babies.

Oddly, we were all surprised by how removed from society we were. Ironically, we got practically no news of the War. The only news we ever got regarding Viet Nam was the news that elements of American Special Forces had attempted the rescue of roughly 70 prisoners of war held at the Son Tay prison in North Viet Nam. Even though the mission failed to rescue a single P.O.W., we rejoiced that "we" had the courage to at least attempt a rescue. We felt a kinship with our P.O.W. "brothers" and with the Special Forces trying to rescue them, a kinship we had not felt just a few days before. For the first time I felt like I was part of something bigger than myself. For the first time I felt like I was part of something important. And, for the first time I felt like I had found my new "home."

Boot camp was not as physically demanding as I had anticipated. While I knew the Navy was not the Marine Corps, I had thought that my purchase of the Ted Williams certified Sears & Roebuck weight set would pay dividends. Navy boot camp was not without its physical challenges. On special occasions my company was visited by one of Chief Clark's "colleagues" when Chief Clark was not around. This was a Gunners Mate First Class who had seen recent service in Viet Nam aboard the battle-ship *New Jersey*. He was on a one-man mission to weed out "fuck-ups." He apparently derived personal entertainment from watching recruits writhing in tears in pools of sweat as we attempted to comply with his physical exercise demands.

We did have two more formalized exercise routines that were "awarded" for minor infractions of the rules. One was known as a "marching party" the other was called a "grass party." The marching party was usually for remedial drill instruction for those that did not take readily to marching and close-order drill with our bolt-action Springfield rifles. Grass parties tended to be reserved for personal failures, like missing a whisker in the crease at the corner of my mouth while shaving one morning. The grass party, which consisted of doing a series of rifle exercises on a beach-sand yard. One of the favorite exercises was holding one's rifle at arm's length in front of one's face for a prolonged period until one vomited.

Chief Clark's "signature" policy was group punishment – "all for one and one for all," so to speak. When one recruit committed an error all of us were held accountable. In Company 202 that meant getting "special" extra short haircuts. In 1970, hair was the most important symbol of our generation. Many recruits had lost shoulder-length hair on Induction Day and it was our goal to regain as much of our lost locks as possible before we reentered the outside world following boot camp graduation. On Induction Day our heads had been shaved. Each subsequent weekly haircut permitted the barber to attach a clip-on devise to his shears that allowed our hair to ultimately gain about one-half inch in length by graduation. Most of us had thrown away our combs in favor of a hair-brush, better to train our short hair. With proper training we could usually achieve a part with roughly an eighth inch of growth. With each of Chief Clark's "specials" we were returned to zero. Getting a "special" became our greatest fear as we got closer to graduation. Thirteen weeks after Induction Day, Company 202 reentered the "real world" – bald. I still use a brush instead of a comb.

Upon departure from boot camp I had the sense that I had finally entered the world of the men I admired the most – the World War II veterans. That was until I got to the Orlando airport. There my fellow boot camp graduates and I were greeted by our first of what would become many confrontations with war protesters. For the first time we were called "baby killers" and we were spat upon. Some of my boot camp compatriots had somehow been able to acquire civilian clothes which they could not throw on fast enough in the airport men's room. Of course, they looked ridiculous in their tie-died dungarees; double-knit wide collared paisley shirts; black spit-shined Navy-issue dress shoes; and two-toned bald heads. (Our faces were partially tanned from wearing our white hats at exactly two fingers width above our eyebrows. The tops of our heads were white and accentuated by the painstakingly brush-trained part on the left side). This was not the picture that I had created from my mother's description of young men returning home during World War Two, a picture in which all the young men were seen proudly, yet casually, wearing their service uniforms in all settings. The exception was the young man who was not wearing a uniform. Those not wearing uniforms were looked upon with curiosity if not pity. Surely something must have been wrong with them.

For the next two weeks after boot camp I avoided appearing in public. It was apparent that I was no longer welcome in my own hometown. The only time I donned my uniform was to visit my maternal grandmother, Bessie Burne. We would begin a ritual that would be repeated for the next seven years until she passed away. Whenever I would return home for a visit I would pay a call on Grammy Burne. Each time I walked into her kitchen, I was greeted by the familiar aroma of freshly baked bread and a big hug. She would take me by the hand and lead me to the living room couch where we would sit and talk about everything I had done since our last meeting. Through her undivided attention, her sincerity, and her unconditional love, I was reassured that what I was doing was honorable and just. I imagined that the reassurance she gave me was the same support she had extended to her own sons and the other neighborhood boys who had gone off to serve during the World War II, Korea and Viet Nam. Her encouragement made me feel like I had taken my place among the people I admired the most. While going home to Westford was never the same after her passing, her encouragement provided me with the strength to persevere in what was to be largely a "thankless" career in the Navy. For my generation of servicemen, military service was one of "invisibility" to virtually everyone outside our immediate families and our extended "military family."

Over the next several years I would increase my distance from my hometown as I immersed myself in the isolation of a service life. My first stop was in a service school in San Diego, a city where the Navy had a massive presence. San Diego was one of the few places a serviceman could go where wearing a uniform was actually encouraged. Servicemen in uniforms could gain discount or even free entry to places like the San Diego Zoo or San Diego Padres baseball games. The Navy had decided that I was to become an Interior Communications (IC for short) Electrician with advanced training in nuclear power for service aboard submarines. I was thrown in with other future "IC men" who were generally older and had more advanced education than I had. In my barracks room of four, all but me had at least two years of college. One, my good friend George Love, had a bachelor's degree. For these men, classes on electricity and electronics were a breeze. For me, it was a struggle. The study habits that had gotten me through high school simply didn't hack it.

Since classes were easy for the majority of the students, our instructors, who were only a few years older than us, took to shortening the lessons and spending a lot of class time screening episodes of the 50's classic documentary television series, *Victory at Sea*. While enlightening, class time spent watching *Victory at Sea* films meant electricity and electronics, in my case, would have to be largely self-taught. I became a

29

nightly customer at the base library where I would immerse myself in textbooks and technical manuals while my roommates were at the base enlisted club drinking beer by the pitcher or at the women's barracks, affectionately referred to as the "WAVE Cage," enticing women into drinking beer with them. The base library would close at 2200 (10 p.m.) while the base club would close at midnight. This routinely resulted with me being rolled out of my bunk by one of my roommates who would return from the club drunk and in need of my wool blanket. On weekends my roommates liked to diversify their alcohol intake by switching to cheap wine. On one particular Saturday night, after consuming the majority of a gallon jug of Boone's Farm Strawberry Hill, one roommate proceeded to vomit the Strawberry Hill, along with the pizza he had consumed, all over our room and bedding. The remainder of the night was spent cleaning and airing our room while the incessantly apologizing roommate looked on helplessly. This event and others like it caused me to question whether I was cut out for enlisted life. Part of my evening ritual at the base library became researching an "escape strategy."

At the time there were two options that seemed to be in common use that enabled my fellow enlisted classmates to leave school prematurely. One was to fail out of school. Each Friday we received a multiple choice test that covered the materials taught during the week. Failure of one of these tests resulted in an immediate "academic review board" in which the student would be told to not fail another test. A second failure would routinely result in immediate dismissal from the school and immediate reassignment to a ship currently on the "gun-line" off of Viet Nam. The second option was for two sailors to visit one of the Navy chaplains at the base chapel. While with the chaplain the two sailors would declare their "strong feelings" for each other. This action was usually enough to receive an immediate discharge due to "medical reasons."

During the early years of the 70s there was little or no stigma attached to discharges of any characterization, honorable or otherwise. The Navy had no problem recruiting volunteers while the Army was still drafting. A third, less used option, was to obtain an assignment to a higher priority program. Through my library research I learned that the only way for me to get assigned to a program with a higher priority than nuclear submarines was to get accepted to the Naval Academy in Annapolis.

Thus began my long and circuitous route to the college I had targeted back in junior high school.

By July of 1971, I was sent to a school removed from the fleet and removed from the ongoing antiwar movement. I was assigned to the Naval Academy Preparatory School located in Bainbridge, Maryland. Bainbridge was a plywood city slapped together during World War II to process and train men, and women for service in the war effort. In 1971 Bainbridge was primarily known for being home of one of the two nuclear power training schools the other being in Vallejo, California. Off in a hidden and secluded corner of the base was the former Tome School, an independent boarding prep school established in 1894. In 1942 Congress had appropriated the Tome School and adjacent farm land to house the Bainbridge Naval Training Center. The Naval Academy Preparatory School would occupy the Tome School facilities until Bainbridge was dissolved in 1976. (The Navy prep school is currently located at the naval station in Newport, Rhode Island). While the original intent of NAPS was to provide remedial college preparatory education and advanced military training to young sailors aspiring to become commissioned officers in the naval service, by 1971 the majority of attendees were recent high school graduates who were promising athletes but needed to improve their academic credentials and standardized test scores prior to being acceptable to the Academy.

As it turned out, NAPS was, for me, exactly what I needed to survive the physical and mental rigors of four years at Annapolis. At NAPS we immersed ourselves in the fundamental subjects of math, English, and science. We all were required to participate in sports, physical fitness, and at least one extra-curricular activity.

For a year we were isolated from the turmoil of the college campuses and the anti-war demonstrations. Ironically, the turmoil had gotten worse after the draft was "improved" in 1969. The new lottery draft was supposed to be random and it was not supposed to discriminate against young men because of their economic, educational or racial status. Apparently, when more affluent better educated young white men realized that their college days may come to an abrupt end by way of a draft notice, the campus protesting boiled over. The lottery draft was to be short-lived. The military draft was abandoned permanently in 1973.

31

For me, there was still a passing interest in the outcome of the 1971 draft lottery. From the student lounge at the NAPS dining hall I watched "my number" drawn. My number was 60. That year draft numbers 1 through 95 were called to serve. I would have been drafted. While it was a moot point for me, this knowledge nevertheless made me feel a kinship with the generation of my father and uncles all of whom were subject to be drafted.

With the exception of the few times I traveled home for holidays, there were very few occasions when I came in contact with the public, but when I did, it was in uniform and I was subjected to the condescending comments and "you baby killer" glares from virtually everyone on the city streets, in bus stations and airport terminals. I guess the low point of this time during the waning days of the draft and of the Viet Nam War came at Christmastime in 1972. I was in my first semester of the dreaded Plebe Year, at the Naval Academy. I traveled home to Westford anticipating a white Christmas and a reunion with family and friends. As part of our family observance of Christmas that year, we attended church services at the First Parish Church United, the Congregational church overlooking Westford's town common. Naturally, I wore my new midshipman's dress blue uniform with the distinctive brass trim of a naval officer. As my luck would have it, President Nixon had ordered what came to be known as the "Christmas Bombings." The bombings, which began on December 18th and continued through the 29th, were carried out by B-52 heavy bombers against targets in North Viet Nam. The bombings were the heaviest bombing campaign since the end of World War Two.

The historic significance of this event was not lost on our church's pastor. Instead of a ministerial message in keeping with the joyous Christian religious holiday, our minister angrily railed against the bombing campaign, much of the time directing his stern gaze and vitriol at the only one in the congregation wearing a military uniform, me. Unlike Dorothy in the Wizard of Oz, clicking her heals and chanting "there's no place like home, there's no place like home," I wanted to click my heals together and go to a place anywhere but home. I left that candlelight service that snowy night bewildered and wondering what had gone wrong. Why was I, a Plebe struggling to get passing grades, to blame for the

War? How was it that Congress, which had overwhelmingly approved of war in the Tonkin Gulf Resolution, escaped the wrath that I was incurring on Christmas Eve 1972? How had the people of my little town turned against the war and turned against its own native sons?

As was the custom during my four years at the Naval Academy, first semester exams were given following the Christmas and New Year break. Aside from my Christmas Eve tongue lashing, my vacation was uneventful and unproductive. Even though I had carried my entire collection of textbooks home with me to study for exams I only made a cursory effort to prepare for the onslaught of exams that would greet me immediately upon return to Annapolis. Exams were a blur. On one particular day I had three exams with the third exam being my worst subject, calculus. I had prepared for the full slate of exams by pulling an "all-nighter". By the time I got to my calculus exam the caffeine had worn off and what little calculus knowledge I had on a good day, escaped completely on this very bad day. I failed.

Following our last semester exam we were permitted to leave Annapolis on "semester break". Although it had only been a little more than a week since returning from Christmas vacation, I elected to catch a ride with an upperclassman in my company (a military unit of around 120 men) who owned a Dodge van and was driving north to Massachusetts. In the early 70s First Class midshipmen (senior upperclassmen) were permitted to own automobiles and keep them at the Academy. During this period the most popular choice of vehicle among midshipmen was the full size van, then commonly referred to as "passion wagons." These vans were usually "customized" with special paint jobs and interiors replete with wall-to-wall shag carpeting, tables, captain's chairs, and 8-track tape players with stereo speakers. In return for gas and toll money lowly underclassmen could usually get rides. Semester break would have been unremarkable but for one historic event – the Paris Peace Accords. The Christmas Bombings had succeeded in getting North Viet Nam to a cessation of hostilities. The Viet Nam War was over, so we thought in January of 1973. My Dad, a Navy ordinance man during World War II, rolled-out an antique miniature cannon and provided a memorable black powder salute to mark the occasion. I reveled in the momentary sensation that the sacrifices of my fellow brothers in arms had not been in vain.

33

I returned to the Naval Academy for the long period between the end of first semester final exams and graduation (the Naval Academy did not observe Spring Break in the early 70s), a period known to midshipmen as The Dark Ages. I was quickly snapped back to the realities of attending the Naval Academy in the early 1970s. While walking back to the Maryland Avenue gate, Gate 3, I was spat upon by a group of what appeared to be male and female college students. Upon entering my wing of the sprawling Academy dormitory building, Bancroft Hall, I had to immediately break into the ritual of "chopping" (running) in the center of the hallways and "sounding off" as I "squared" each corner. The third and final insult came when I saw the exam scores posted on the wall outside our company's office. Although I had known I had failed my calculus final, seeing it on the computer printout confirmed in my mind that "there would be consequences."

Even though the Dark Ages of 1973 was living up to its reputation, one event that occurred during this period would cement itself in my memory as one of the most emotional events of my life – the return of the P.O.W.s. Beginning in February 1973, in what was referred to as Operation Homecoming, American prisoners of war were released from prison camps in North Viet Nam. Primarily made up of Navy and Air Force aviators, prisoners had been held captive since 1964. Many of the naval aviator prisoners happened to be Naval Academy graduates.

On one particular day the 4000-man Brigade of Midshipmen was assembled, like every other day, in the dining hall, King Hall, to sit down for the noon meal. Each meal was preceded by a brief prayer and announcements read by the Brigade Commander, the highest ranking midshipman. Occasionally the Brigade Commander would announce a special guest of the Brigade joining him at the head table of this cavernous "T" shaped dining hall. On rare occasions the guest would be someone famous. For these special guests upper-class midshipmen would order Plebes, like army ants, to descend on this unsuspecting guest and hoist him, still in his dinner chair, above their shoulders and parade the guest up and down each wing of the dining hall to the applause and cheers of the entire Brigade.

On this day, the Brigade Commander announced that we were joined by the Navy P.O.W.s. Spontaneously, the entire Plebe Class of

1976 bolted from our tables and descended on these most special of guests, our returned heroes. While I cannot say who it was that I carried on my right shoulder that day, I do remember him to be old before his time; prematurely grey; and, much lighter than one would expect a six-foot-tall man to be. I remember cheering and crying at the same time. A brief glance into the eyes of the man riding above our shoulders confirmed that he was crying as well. Although I would not graduate until after the final American unceremoniously escaped Saigon, this single event made me feel connected with the thankless heroes of Viet Nam. This single event would sustain me for the remainder of the dark years of the 70s, years in which the military, instead of the government, was held account-able for what was to be assessed as a "failed war."

After Viet Nam

1973 would prove to be an eventful year for our future as professional naval officers. The return of the P.O.W.s appeared to mark the end of the country's and the government's attention span relative to Viet Nam, even though the American military would be heavily involved in the conflict for two more years culminating with the final desperate evacuation of Saigon and the ensuing brutalization of the people of South Viet Nam. Shortly after the joyous return of the P.O.W.s, the national attention shifted to the Watergate Scandal. This scandal resulted from a politically moti-vated botched burglary during the 1972 presidential campaign. As a result of Watergate the president was seriously undermined in his role as Commander in Chief. Congress was emboldened to take action not only in response to Watergate but also in response to Viet Nam and the war powers of the president. In late 1973, the Congress passed and then over-rode President Nixon's veto of the War Powers Resolution. The War Powers Act would be the legislative response to the two protracted, un-declared, wars since World War II - Korea and Viet Nam. The War Pow-ers Resolution and the Tonkin Gulf Resolution before it would affect the way in which the United States fights wars, henceforward. To add to the atmosphere of scandal and loss of trust, Vice President Agnew became the second vice president in history to resign from office.

For the next three years I was more concerned about getting and keeping my grade point average above 2.0 and struggling to learn Mandarin Chinese than I was with the national drama being played out 30 miles down U.S. Route 50 in Washington, D.C. By the second semester of my senior year I was looking forward to graduation and finally taking my place in the fleet as a surface warfare officer. One of my diversions at the Academy was as an organizer of popular music concerts for the midshipmen. On one concert weekend I had the pleasure of escorting Charlie Daniels. Ostensibly to avoid crowd control problems, mainly with bands that had a large "groupie" following, senior midshipmen would pick up performing artists at their hotels and drive them unnoticed through the streets of Annapolis and into the Academy yard to the concert venue in the Halsey Field House. This night I picked up Mr. Daniels at the Howard Johnson Motor Lodge on the outskirts of the city. During the drive in Mr. Daniels was telling me about a great new presidential candidate that he was backing, Jimmy Carter. I don't know whether Mr. Daniels knew it before I told him but our conversation became more animated when I told him that Jimmy Carter was a Naval Academy graduate, Class of 1947. By the end of the night Charlie Daniels had convinced me to vote for Jimmy Carter.

At first, we Naval Academy graduates assumed that we were electing a friend of the Navy, someone who had "walked the walk." To our dismay, Jimmy Carter became anything but an inspiring Commander in Chief to lead us out of the "shame" of Watergate and the years immediately following the fall of Viet Nam.

The period of the mid-70s was a period of transition and adaptation for those of us in the military. It appeared that the election of Jimmy Carter was a way for the people to "turn the page" and leave the "unpleasantness" of Viet Nam behind. The newly elected government seemed more than willing to oblige the people by placing the blame for the war squarely on the men sent to fight the war. The policy makers and legislators who so enthusiastically passed the Tonkin Gulf Resolution ten years earlier were content to let the military languish in a state of low morale and degraded readiness. While the impact of the War Powers Resolution of 1973 would not be felt for several years to come, the impact of force reductions and the end of the draft were beginning to be felt.

During my final year at the Naval Academy one of the most important decisions I had to make was referred to as "service selection." Service selection was when we got to choose what part of the naval service we were to serve in, conceivably for the better part of our adult lives. For my all-male class this meant choosing service as an aviator, submariner, surface warfare officer, or in the marines. There were prerequisites and quotas for all selections. Service selection was also determined by one's order of merit, also known as class standing. In theory, the higher the class standing was, the better the job and the greater the likelihood of a successful career.

I had trouble deciding what I wanted be. I considered becoming a marine pilot, but unlike my roommate, Stephen Hastings, I had not dreamed of becoming a marine my entire life. When I discovered that my selection of Marine Corps would mean a fellow classmate of lower class standing would be deprived a slot he had been dreaming about since childhood, I decided to go with my "gut" and chose a surface ship. I picked my first ship based on "good looks." For four years I had passed by a scale model of the *USS Luce* in the foyer of the Academy's Luce Hall, the seamanship and navigation training building. *Luce* was a guided missile destroyer with especially sleek and classic lines, and above all, she was a worthy descendent of the "tin cans" of World War II.

I made up a short list of the guided missile destroyers of the *Luce* Class for the purpose of preparing for my service selection. Working in my favor, all of the Class was home-ported on the east coast. (I would later learn that this was because the Class had the worst fuel efficiency in the fleet. They were all located on the east coast to avoid the longer, more costly, transits of the Pacific Ocean). Doubly in my favor, most of them were in Norfolk, regarded by many Naval Academy midshipmen as "Shit City." (Most midshipmen at the time wanted assignments to the more glamorous ports of San Diego or Pearl Harbor). I chose USS Coontz (DDG-40) home-ported in Norfolk. On the advice of my surface warfare officer mentors at the Academy I should choose a billet in operations or weapons. I should avoid engineering at all costs. (Engineering department officers, also known as "snipes," worked ungodly hours, under arduous if not dangerous conditions. Furthermore, "engineers" were not well aligned career-wise for ascension to the rank of admiral). Coontz had a billet open in weapons as the missile officer, the "sexiest" job on the entire ship. I was a "made" man, so I thought.

The remaining six months at the Academy were a blur. Before I knew it I was packing all my uniforms into the back of my bright orange Saab 99 and I was headed down the coast to Guided Missile School in Dam Neck, Virginia. I arrived in Virginia Beach, lost and exhausted, on July 4th 1976, the Bicentennial. I pulled into the first motel I could find and crashed for the night. I totally missed out on the festivities of the day. The next morning, a Monday, I reported in to Guided Missile School. To my surprise I was one of three officers in the class of about a dozen who had orders to "my ship," Coontz, and I was the junior man. My first day in the "real" Navy, and my career was a wreck, my path to admiral in serious jeopardy.

Shortly after immersing myself into the world of guided missiles and fire control radars I, and the other two members of my class slated to serve aboard Coontz were summoned one evening to the home of the ship's Executive Officer. To our surprise the ship's Commanding Officer was also in attendance. The XO and CO greeted us by serving us a round of ice cold peppermint schnapps with a beer chaser. It was clear that the XO and CO had already had one or two rounds of this combination before we arrived. After being regaled with stories from a recently completed six-month deployment to the North Atlantic as part of a NATO squadron, we got down to the business at hand, determining the course of my career.

My Captain was a beloved commanding officer. His baritone voice was finely honed by his chain smoking. His rosy complexion was punctuated by a W.C. Fields-like nose that advertised his tendency to consume copious quantities of alcohol. In 1976 much of the Navy was still trying to live up to its reputation for heavy drinking and heavy smoking. In the eyes of his adoring crew the Captain was simply upholding tradition. My Captain also had a great sense of humor. With a straight face and solemn voice he explained that he planned to assign me the duties of - Athletic Officer. My mind flashed immediately to the character in my favorite movie "Mr. Roberts" starring Henry Fonda. In the movie Jack Lemmon portrays the bumbling Ensign Pulver who is assigned as the ship's Laundry Officer. Was I being "groomed" to be the ship's laughing stock like Ensign Pulver?

After having a good laugh at my expense my Captain explained to me that I would be initially assigned as the Assistant Combat Information Center Officer but that his plan was for me to eventually become the DCA, short for Damage Control Assistant. The DCA was one of the two principal assistants to the ship's Chief Engineer (the other being the MPA, or, Main Propulsion Assistant) and is responsible for virtually all engineering related equipment and personnel outside of the ship's main propulsion spaces. In Coontz this would mean I was responsible for all matters relating to anything bad that can happen to a ship at sea, like fires, floods, thermonuclear explosions and clogged toilets. Translation – the least "sexy" job on the ship. The large division of men I would eventually lead was made up of Hull Technicians, Electricians, Interior Communications Electricians, Machinist Mates, Machinery Repairmen, and Enginemen. Many of the men were castoffs from the main spaces, the fire rooms and engine rooms, and were derisively known among engineers as "fresh air snipes." While putting on a brave face at the time, I realized that being assigned as DCA was tantamount to a condemnation to career hell. I was going to be an "engineer."

Being told that I was not going to be a "shooter" aboard Coontz did not do my classroom attentiveness at Guided Missile School very much good. I struggled to pass the course. Nevertheless I made the most of my summer assignment to the Navy's beachfront station by acquiring an excellent tan and establishing a "social life" that I had not enjoyed, well, ever, but especially at the Naval Academy. On one particular night I and two other junior officers were "dragged" by the senior officer in our missile school class, Lieutenant Commander Jim Bates, to a weekly social event known as "Sing Along" at the Little Creek Amphibious Base. "Sing Along" consisted of singing traditional, mostly navy, songs led by the "legendary" piano player named "Pappy." Sing Along was also popular because on this night of the week young ladies from the Hampton Roads area attended. Wishing to make light conversation with women half his age, Jim Bates ordered (dared) me to invite two young women who had just entered the room to join our table. One of those two young ladies would eventually become my wife. In very short order since leaving Annapolis, my career had taken an ominous turn yet my life had improved immeasurably.

Over the next four years aboard Coontz I entered a career in which I had a front-row seat to the Cold War with the Soviet Union; I personally witnessed the transformation from a draft-influenced military to the "all volunteer force" of the present day; I experienced Congressionally mandated social engineering and affirmative action in the military; I watched the post-Viet Nam "rebirth" of the military under Ronald Reagan; I endured the consequences of the "peace dividend" under George H.W. Bush and Bill Clinton following the demise of the Soviet Union; and, I observed the ever-widening crevasse between the American military and the American people.

For the most part my career in the Navy was served in anonymity. With the exception of a brief period in 1983 when my ship's mission off the coast of Nicaragua was documented in the pages of Newsweek magazine, no one in my family, other than my wife and two-year-old daughter, knew any more than I was "out." We had entered a period when essentially the only people that knew or cared about the whereabouts and activities of service men and women are the service men and women themselves and their immediate families. Aside from the occasional perfunctory platitudes of politicians and members of the media, the daily sacrifices and trials faced by members of the extended "military family" are invisible to the American public.

It would not be until several years later, as I was preparing to teach my university class on the subject of war that I delved into the "science" of war according to Clausewitz and Corbett. Only then did I begin to comprehend and appreciate what I had experienced and what I am observing in the present. It has caused me to question the way in which we have entered into and conducted war since the end of World War II. I have concluded that it is **no way to fight a war**.

Prussian General Carl von Clausewitz and British naval historian, Sir Julian Corbett have led me to conclude that we are in "violation" of several precepts of war fighting. The precepts spelled out by Clausewitz and Corbett further reinforced for me the words of my childhood hero, General Douglas MacArthur: "In war, there is no substitute for victory." Clausewitz and Corbett also clarified for me the wisdom of General MacArthur when he advised against engaging in a land war in Southeast Asia. Clausewitz and Corbett provided me with a springboard to better understanding my own concerns about the dissolution of the military draft. Furthermore, they provided me with a greater respect for our Constitution and its role in providing for our national security and the vital importance of the separation of powers devised by the Constitution's framers.

We The People at War – Applying the Trinity Theory

General Carl von Clausewitz
Reproduced with the permission of The Clausewitz Homepage

Clausewitz

I am not a Clausewitz scholar by any stretch. I am amused by the dispute among Clausewitz "scholars" about virtually every aspect of Clausewitz's life and observations, even his name. My preference is to side with the claims of both Clausewitz and his wife, Marie, in assigning to him Carl Philipp Gottfried von Clausewitz as his full name.

Carl von Clausewitz, like the great public policy theorist,

Machiavelli, suffers from oversimplification and misinterpretation. Very often Clausewitz is dismissively and derisively distilled to one quote from the posthumously compiled Vom Kriege (On War): "War is merely the continuation of policy by other means." When taken in isolation this "signature" phrase appears to indicate a rather cavalier approach to the subject of war. An even cursory review of Clausewitz's observations related to the subject of war leads one to conclude that Clausewitz is anything but cavalier about war. Only someone who is predisposed toward regarding war as an illegitimate method for resolving differences would dismiss Clausewitz's observations on the subject of war.

Why do I think Clausewitz is important to our understanding of American war policy? After all, Clausewitz wrote down his observations related to war during the first part of the 19th Century. How could he be relevant?

First, Clausewitz had experience. He entered military life in 1792 at the age of 12. He went on to serve in various capacities primarily in the Prussian Army. When not engaged in battle he was deeply involved in military education, most notably, as director of the war college in Berlin from 1818 to 1830. During his 12 years at the war college he immersed himself in the study of war and all its facets. While he did not publish any of his research at the time, he told his wife, Marie, that he would leave the publication of his work to her following his death. In 1830, Major General Clausewitz was appointed chief of staff of the Prussian Army and was posted to the border with Poland with the mission of "containing" the Polish Revolution. In 1831 he contracted cholera while serving on the battlefield. He died on November 16th of that year. Beginning in 1832 and culminating in 1837, Marie, fulfilling her husband's prescient earlier remarks to her, collected his incomplete observations on the subject of war and published *Vom Kriege*.

Clausewitz combined both practical experience and scholarship. While he died an untimely death before completing his research, his apparent desire to be published posthumously indicates to me a special humility lacking in contemporary scholars. The fact that Clausewitz was neither looking to enhance his personal fame nor to enrich himself seems to lend to the credibility and value of his work.

Clausewitz was, in the eyes of some 20th Century historians, to blame in part for the two wars of German aggression and for that reason was largely discounted by military practitioners of the early and mid 20th

Century. Beginning in 1976 though, Clausewitz gained considerable favor, especially in the American military. Clausewitz is now the basis for most theoretic studies of war in all branches of the military. For example, *Warfighting: The U.S. Marine Corps Book of Strategy* compiled under the leadership of Commandant, General A.M. Gray and first published in 1989, is largely based on the work of Clausewitz.

Clausewitz's war fighting experience and observations are based on his experience as an infantry officer. His experience predates armor and air combat. He does not address the role of naval forces in the prosecution of combat operations or at least he did not address sea power prior to his death. However, from my standpoint as a former naval officer, as a university instructor, and as a concerned father of a Marine Corps officer, Clausewitz manages to explain war better than anyone before or since the publication of *Vom Kriege*. Much of what he says strikes the reader as common sense, at least until you realize that no one before or since Clausewitz has done a better job.

For the purposes of my observations on the prosecution of war by the United States since World War II, I limit my venture into Clausewitz "scholarship" to Clausewitz's "Trinity Theory." In the concluding section of Chapter I, Book I – On the Nature of War. Clausewitz summarizes his "wonderful (also widely translated as "remarkable") trinity" of war:

> War is, therefore, not only a true chameleon, because it changes its nature in some degree in each particular case, but it is also, as a whole, in relation to the predominant tendencies which are in it, a wonderful trinity, composed of the original violence of its elements, hatred and animosity, which may be looked upon as blind instinct; of the play of probabilities and chance, which make it a free activity of the soul; and of the subordinate nature of a political instrument, by which it belongs purely to the reason.

> The first of these three phases concerns more the people; the second more the general and his army; the third more the Government. The passions which break forth in war must already have a latent existence in the peoples. The range which the display of courage and tal-

43

ents shall get in the realm of probabilities and of chance depends on the particular characteristics of the general and his army; but the political objects belong to the Government alone.

These three tendencies, which appear like so many different lawgivers, are deeply rooted in the nature of the subject, and at the same time variable in degree. A theory which would leave any one of them out of account, or set up any arbitrary relation between them, would immediately become involved in such a contradiction with the reality, that it might be regarded as destroyed at once by that alone.

The problem is, therefore, that theory shall keep itself poised in a manner between these three tendencies, as between three points of attraction.

It seems to me that Clausewitz in a simple, yet elegant, way explains the nature of war by defining war by assigning it three interdependent and coequal elements, "hatred and animosity (or blind instinct)," "the play of probabilities and chance," and "the subordinate nature of a political instrument." In turn he links these elements with three fundamental entities within a nation state. He connects the element of hatred and animosity with the people, or citizens, of a nation. The element of probability and chance is assigned to the military, the entity that must perform under the ever changing, chameleon-like, conditions of armed conflict. The political instrument, from which the policy-seed of war is derived, is assigned to the nation's government.

Clausewitz's "Trinity Theory" is made more critical for the United States because of the fact that the foundation upon which the Constitution rests is – We the People. All actions by a government and its instruments are performed with the direct or indirect consent and for the benefit of, The People. I view Clausewitz's trinity as being like a three-legged stool; war cannot stand without its "three legs" holding it up. Herein lies the first major failing of American war fighting since World War II – We the People are largely left out of the picture.

During World War II, President Roosevelt and other members of the national government at that time seem to have been acutely aware of the importance of including "the people" as equal partners in the war effort. Seemingly small measures such as gas and food rationing; neighborhood watch organizations; and, war bond sales served to complement the huge contribution made in human terms by the people through the military draft. According to Selective Service records, during World War II over 10 million men were drafted, roughly 7 percent of the nation'spopulation in 1940. A total of around 16 million men and women served in the military during the course of the war, or roughly 12 percent of the total population of about 132 million in 1940.

In contrast to the World War II effort, during the Korean Conflict between 1950 and 1953 only slightly more than 1.5 million men were drafted, roughly one percent of the total population. During the Viet Nam War, roughly 1.8 million men were drafted between 1964 and 1973, a total slightly less than one percent of the nation's population at the time. Under the all volunteer military that in 2009 is engaged in armed conflict around the world associated with the War on Terror, the active force of around 1.6 million is approximately one half of one percent of the nation's current population of around 305 million. The combined total of all active and reserve forces along with all surviving veterans, is around 8 percent of the population, slightly more than the percentage of draftees during World War II alone.

Following the Pearl Harbor attack in late 1941, President Roosevelt and the Congress, while tapping into the "hatred and animosity" felt by the people following the surprise attack of Sunday morning, December 7th, strictly adhered to the dictates of the Constitution. Congress formally declaring war in accordance with its enumerated powers under Section 8 of Article I [Appendix I] while the president conformed to his power as Commander in Chief of the armed forces granted in Section 2 of Article II. The two branches of government worked closely for the remainder of the war until a total defeat of the enemy was achieved. It would appear that an equal partnership among the military, the government and the people provided the necessary war footing to sustain the war effort, even following setbacks and mounting casualties.

During World War II, few families were untouched by the fear and uncertainty of the war. Virtually all families of young men went to sleep at night wondering where their sons and brothers were and whether

45

they were in harm's way. Conversations among neighbors invariably centered on the latest war news or a recent letter from some far off place. Every community made up a "support group." A full range of emotions - anxiety, grief, joy - were shared among everyone.

Besides the aforementioned difference in draft numbers, the wars subsequent to World War II engaged in by the United States have been far different in other respects. The most glaring difference is that Congress has failed to "declare war" in accordance with its obligations under Article I of the Constitution. Since World War II no president has asked for and no Congress has insisted upon a formal declaration. Why not? While I could find some excuses I can find no clear reasons for not declaring war. Certainly armed conflicts subsequent to World War II have been costly in terms of American blood and treasure. Certainly a young marine killed at Chosin, Khe Sanh, or Fallujah is as dead as the young soldier killed at Normandy.

A reading of the Federalist Papers on the matter of war declaration indicates that the framers of the Constitution left the subject intentionally vague. There is no format given for what a declaration of war should look like. There is no definition of what sort of war required a declaration and what sort did not. One thing is very clear though, the framers intentionally separated the power to declare war from the power to wage war. It is also my sense that the framers regarded a declaration of war as an act of great gravity and importance. A vote for declaration of war was to be a sacred act, a "crossing of the Rubicon" undertaking from which the nation cannot turn back. A declaration of war was intended to be a commitment of the government on behalf of the people to support the military until victory was achieved. The framers understood from their own recent experience with war that in war there is no room for half measures. All necessary power must be vested in the Executive in order to contend with what Clausewitz referred to as the "chameleon-like" nature of warfare. In war there is no substitute for victory.

By failing to declare war the Congress, and by extension, the people of the United States have been removed from the decision making process of when to go to war, and, more importantly, when not to. A failure to declare war has weakened the commitment of the government and the people to support the military until victory is achieved.

Limited War

Sir Julian S. Corbett
Courtesy of Project Gutenberg

Corbett

Sir Julian Stafford Corbett was born in 1854. He attended Cambridge University and entered a career in the law following graduation. In 1882 he retired from his law career. Following his passion for history, he began a second career in which he traveled widely and wrote historical novels. In 1896 he was asked to become involved with a project documenting the Spanish War that culminated in 1588 with the near complete destruction of the Spanish Armada. This project effectively launched, at midlife, a new career as a naval historian. He went on to become an influential force within the Royal Navy, lecturing regularly at the British Naval War College shortly after it was founded in 1900.

Corbett came to his knowledge of warfare through reading and research, never gaining the firsthand wartime experience advocated by his "hero," Clausewitz. Although Corbett's main contribution is as a naval warfare theorist and strategist, in his 1911 book, *Some Principles of Maritime Strategy*, he provides us with a critical "missing link" between Clausewitz and modern warfare strategy – he completed Clausewitz's unfinished work on "limited war."

Corbett's explanation of limited war allows us to more fully understand the United States war strategy of the modern age. Since the end of World War II and the dawning of the Nuclear Age, the United States has pursued a strategy of limited war in every armed conflict from Korea to the present day. Corbett's incites explain how the United States, its allies and the United Nations could have avoided the inconclusive Korean War; how the failure in Viet Nam could have been avoided; and, how similar mistakes in strategy could have been avoided in Iraq and Afghanistan.

In the years immediately preceding his death Clausewitz was laboring to explain forms of warfare that were something short of his "ideal" form, or, "absolute war." Heretofore, Clausewitz was a proponent of fighting war with only one objective in mind – the complete destruction of the army of an opponent and the causing of the opponent's government to give into the "will" of its conqueror. The outcome of this absolute war was conclusive and usually resulted in the annexation of territory or the dissolution of entire countries. Clausewitz had come to this conclusion through observation and firsthand participation in the European continental wars of the Napoleonic Era. However, in the latter stages of the Napoleonic wars events on the ground apparently caused Clausewitz to modify his theories. He needed to account for how smaller or inferior armies such as that of Britain could defeat the larger, seemingly superior, armies such as that of Napoleon at Waterloo. He also needed to account for the outcome of Waterloo which rather than the dissolution of France resulted in the final surrender and exile of Napoleon and the restoration of Louis XVIII to the French throne. As it would turn out, the capture of Napoleon as he tried to escape, supposedly to North America following the French defeat, would provide an ironic solution to Clausewitz's hunt for an explanation.

Napoleon was captured by a ship of the Royal Navy that was participating in a blockade of the French coast. The Royal Navy was able to "command the seas" along the French coast and was thereby able to limit the options open to Napoleon as well as defending the British Isles from a possible cross-channel attack by the French under Napoleon. The significance of the role of the naval forces was not lost on Corbett, nearly one hundred years later.

Toward the end of his life, Clausewitz was wrestling with the concept of "limited" warfare. He was trying to explain that there could be decisive warfare short of the total conquest of his "absolute" or, "unlimited" war. He concluded that if there was a "limited objective" to a war or there was a "limited contingent" (limited size of the armed force used) there would necessarily be an outcome that was somewhat short of total defeat of an enemy. It was possible for a country to pursue wars without having designs on acquiring new territory or annexing other countries and other peoples. Due to Clausewitz's untimely death it was left to Corbett to explain how this was possible.

In Chapter 3 of *Some Principles* Corbett begins his explanation of "limited" verses "unlimited" war by introducing his twist to what Clausewitz had theorized.

> Whatever the object, the vital and paramount question was the intensity with which the spirit of the nation was absorbed in its attainment. The real point to determine in approaching any war plan was what did the object mean to the two belligerents, what sacrifices would they make for it, what risks were they prepared to run? It was thus he stated his view. "The smaller the sacrifice we demand from our opponent, the smaller presumably will be the means of resistance he will employ, and the smaller his means, the smaller will ours be required to be. Similarly the smaller our political object, the less value shall we set upon it and the more easily we shall be induced to abandon it." Thus the political object of the war, its original motive, will not only determine for both belligerents reciprocally the aim of the force they use, but it will also be the standard of the intensity of the efforts they will make. So he concludes there may be wars of all degrees of importance and energy from a war of extermination down to the use of an army of observation. So also in the

49

naval sphere there may be a life and death struggle for maritime supremacy or hostilities which never rise beyond a blockade.

Clausewitz, aided by Corbett, tells us that limited war can fit into a virtually infinite set of circumstances short of wars in which both sides seek to destroy the war fighting capacity of the other. Within these circumstances the degree of effort expended is determined by how much the attacking force wishes to achieve its limited goal as well as by how much the defending force wishes to prevent the limited goal from being achieved.

(At this point it is worthwhile to identify another observation by Clausewitz that is relevant to the discussion of limited war and that has to do with a conflict between powerful forces against much less powerful forces. Clausewitz points out those less powerful forces can achieve an advantage over a more powerful force by "wearing down" the more powerful forces. This is done by making the powerful forces exceed the limits of "blood and treasure" the more powerful force is willing to expend in order to achieve its limited political object for war. This aspect of waging limited war becomes very important to fully understanding the American experience in Viet Nam, the Soviet experience in Afghanistan, and the American experience in Iraq).

Clausewitz stab at explaining limited war was still limited by his limited scope of experience with war. Clausewitz envisioned the limited object to be limited territorial conquest between continental European powers. Further, he believed this limited conquest to be useful primarily as a means of acquiring bargaining chips to get the opposing force's government to agree to some predetermined limited object. This is where the expanded world view of Corbett comes into play in more fully explaining Clausewitz's conundrum. In Corbett's words –

> Standing at the final point which Clausewitz and Jomini reached, we are indeed only on the threshold of the subject. We have to begin where they left off and inquire what their ideas have to tell for the modern conditions of worldwide imperial States, where the sea becomes a direct and vital factor.

In Chapter Four of *Some Principles* Corbett breaks into his full stride in explaining the true nature of limited war. Corbett begins by showing that the Clausewitz vision of limited war is not truly limited. While a corner of a European country might appear to be a limited object for conquest, Corbett points out that the object has the potential for expanding into an unlimited object if country being attacked is willing to expend unlimited resources to defend the seemingly limited the object of the offensive power. He theorized that the continental model always had the potential for degenerating from limited to unlimited in scope.

While conceding Clausewitz's point that the limited war depends on the "geographical position of the object," he takes the theory to the next level by explaining that:

> Firstly, it must be not merely limited in area, but of really limited political importance; and secondly, it must be so situated as to be strategically isolated or to be capable of being reduced to practical isolation by strategical operations.

In other words, Corbett contends that in order to engage in limited warfare not only must the area in which the fighting is to occur limited but it also must be of limited political importance. Perhaps most importantly to Corbett's analysis is that the limited object must be strategically isolated. He contends that limited war is not possible between contiguous states, such as the United States and Canada or the United States and Mexico. While war between contiguous states may use limited armed forces there will always be the possibility of the war between contiguous states that start as a limited engagement, to escalate to an unlimited engagement.

Corbett's statement about "practical isolation by strategic operations" is also a key to understanding how limited war can be carried out. Practical isolation can only apply under certain geographic conditions and in Corbett's view can only be achieved through the employment of naval forces commanding the seas in and around the vicinity of the limited area of hostilities. In Corbett's eyes, limited war can only be effectively employed in the case of an island or a peninsula around which the

51

sea communications can be controlled. Only with the control of transit in and out of the war zone can limited warfare be ultimately successful.

The only ideal limited war can be executed on an island since on a peninsula success is dependent on the territory contiguous with the peninsula. As stated earlier, limited warfare is not possible between contiguous states without the risk of descending into a state of being unlimited.

A second necessity of achieving practical isolation is for the naval power to be not only capable of isolating the location of hostilities, but also it must be able to adequately defend its homeland. This is how Corbett explains the success of the British Empire. The Royal Navy was capable of supporting limited war around the world with the use of limited numbers of ground forces while at the same time preventing a successful assault on the British homeland. During the expansion of the British Empire, limited war was employed successfully to expand colonies around the world. Virtually all British colonies were connected to the sea and were geographically isolatable by the employment of naval forces or by geographic features such as rivers and mountain ranges. In all cases, the colonies were remote from the British homeland; the homeland was secured by the sufficient naval force in reserve for homeland protection; and, the political necessity of establishing the colony was limited, the survival of Britain was not dependent on the success or failure of colonization. Britain could always simply "collect its marbles" and go home.

From this observation Corbett concludes that -

> "...limited war is only permanently possible to island Powers or between Powers which are separated by sea, and then only when the Power desiring limited war is able to command the sea to such a degree as to be able not only to isolate the distant object, but also to render impossible the invasion of his home territory."

Corbett's conclusion explains how it was possible for Britain to create a global empire and how it was able to defeat larger, more populous countries. Britain is an island power separated from all other powers by the sea. Britain's geography plus her command of the seas provide the two necessary elements to wage limited war.

One could argue that, "of course this is what Corbett would say," he was, after all, British and he was a naval historian. He could have been simply trying to curry favor with his bosses at the British Naval War College. History, however, would seem to indicate that Corbett was interested in more than job security. Was he right?

Some Principles of Maritime Strategy, like *Von Kriege*, was largely forgotten and overlooked for much of the 20th Century. The two world wars that dominated the first half of the century tended to follow Clausewitz's original theories related to "absolute war" or unlimited warfare. Among some post-war historians and academic scholars, Clausewitz was partly to blame for the two wars of German aggression. As a result, theorists like Clausewitz and Corbett were largely discounted until very recently. Even to this day, while Clausewitz's reputation has been largely resurrected, Corbett remains a fairly obscure figure. Certainly, as we will see, lessons learned from Corbett have gone unheeded if not totally ignored.

The United States and Limited War

Using Corbett's "discovery" about the nature of limited war a mathematician could formulate an algorithm to help decide whether or not a given political object fit the definition of limited war. A computer scientist could devise a logic diagram with its various "gates" in which to plug-and-chug the numbers and the variables to determine whether or not limited war was possible. Since I am neither a mathematician nor a computer scientist I will simply try to apply common sense to the application of Corbett's rules of limited war. Like a mathematic formula, Corbett's findings consist of both constants and variables. There is a separate set of constants and variables for either side of a limited conflict, one for the expeditionary (offensive) side and one for the objective (defensive) side.

The following is a review of the constants and variables that Corbett asserts are essential in the "object" of limited war.

Constants:

· *Remote object* – The territorial object of limited war must be re-
motely located as opposed to being contiguous with the expeditionary power, the more remote the better. Remoteness provides
for lower probability that forces of the object territory's military
can threaten the expeditionary force's homeland.
· *Sea-girt* – The territorial object is "in touch with the sea." Ide-
ally, the territorial object is surrounded by the sea. At the very
least it is vital that the object is a peninsula that lends itself to
being strategically isolated through the use of naval (and air)
forces.

Variables:

· *No Command of the Sea* – The object's navy is incapable of defending the object in its own territorial sea much less take the
fight to the expeditionary force's home waters.
· *Limited object* – There must be some limited object short of total
conquest and or annexation of the object territory and population. The limited object varies depending on the expense to the
expeditionary power in terms of "blood and treasure" to achieve
its limited objective.
· *Antagonistic behavior* – Something in the object's behavior must
bring about a "popular repugnance" in the people of the expeditionary force. There needs to be a reason for attacking in the first
place, a reason that brings about a willingness, or necessity, on
the part of the people to expend "blood and treasure" in order to
achieve the limited objective.
· *Strategically isolatable* – If the territorial object is not an island,
the territory must be isolatable by controlling all bordering territories. Bordering powers must either be cooperative with the objectives of the expeditionary power or must be isolated from influencing hostilities between the object and the expeditionary
force.

For the expeditionary power the constants and variables are somewhat different. The expeditionary power must have the wherewithal to
transport a fighting force to a remote location with sufficient strength to

achieve a limited objective and sustain operations for an indefinite period of time. The time variable is determined by two factors. The amount of "blood and treasure" the object power is willing to expend in preventing the expeditionary force from achieving its limited objective as well as by the amount of "blood and treasure" the expeditionary power is willing to expend in achieving the limited objective. This is what Clausewitz refers to as the "reciprocal nature of war." The actions and reactions between the belligerents determine the cost and duration of a war and are largely unpredictable. The constants and variables Corbett deems essential for the expeditionary power are:

Constants:

- *Island power* – The expeditionary power must be an island nation. By definition, islands are remote from any potential object of hostile action. Island powers have direct and unchallenged access to the sea.
- *Command of the Seas (and Air)* – The island nation must be able to command the seas around its own territorial waters and if it wishes to take part in limited war must also be able to command the seas around the territorial object of the limited war. In modern warfare it can be assumed that command of the seas by naval forces must also be accompanied by command of the air space over the homeland as well as the territorial object. Command of the sea and air space around the object enables the strategic isolation of the object.

Variables:

- *Limited object* – The expeditionary power must have a limited goal short of conquest and annexation of territory. Unlike in "absolute" or unlimited war, limited war does not necessarily seek to completely overthrow the war fighting capability of the object. The limited object limits the amount of death and destruction to coerce a limited capitulation on the part of the object power. A limited object implies a limited cost as well as a limited duration of hostilities, although of an indeterminate nature. Limited object also implies the use of a limited contingent (armed force). With a limited contingent the expeditionary power must be able to use a fraction of its total armed forces in order to achieve its limited objective. A sufficient reserve force must be withheld from the limited war in order to insure the protection of the homeland and to respond to unforeseen contingency operations that may be required during the involvement with the limited expeditionary action.

· *Popular repugnance* – Also referred by Clausewitz as, the "hatred and animosity" of the people, this is the element that must exist in the expeditionary power's people in order for the "trinity" to be complete. Something about the actions or behavior of the object power must bring about a desire on the part of the expeditionary power to go to war over it. Popular repugnance varies with the limited nature of the object, the more serious the "crime" supposedly the stronger the repugnance. Repugnance will vary according, not only to the severity but also according to the nature and duration of the crime. The nature of the repugnance can be shaped by general prejudices influenced by matters such as ethnicity, race, and religion. Duration of repugnance can be difficult to sustain over long periods of time and is most likely going to be inversely proportionate to time – the longer the duration of war the greater the loss of the people's repugnance.

So how do the actions of the United States stack up to Corbett's tests? Do the objects of limited wars entered into by the United States since the Second World War meet Corbett's requirements? Applying these simple "thumb rules," did Korea, Viet Nam, Iraq and Afghanistan "qualify" as candidates for limited war?

For the United States, two elements of the limited war equation have remained constant over the post-Second World War period. The United States with its friendly neighbors Canada and Mexico, for all intents in purposes, is an Island Power. It is essentially surrounded by two vast oceans that provide nearly unchallenged access to the sea for the purpose of commerce and defense. Virtually any potential adversary fulfills the requirement for being "remote." Since the defeat of the Japanese Navy, and to a lesser extent the German Navy, during the Second World War the United States Navy and United States Air Force have retained command of the seas and air adjacent to the North American continent. While challenged during the Cold War by naval and air forces of the Soviet Union, most notably during the 70s and 80s, the command of the seas and air spaces critical to United States national interests has remained a "constant." So, when it comes to evaluating whether or not the United States is capable of limited war, clearly, since the end of the Second World War, the United States is the only nation capable of engaging in limited warfare. There are no other "island powers" that possess sufficient sea and air power to sustain limited war in remote locations. What then remains to be analyzed are the two variables of "limited object" and "popular repugnance" along with the characteristics of the limited objects themselves, Korea, Viet Nam, Iraq and Afghanistan.

Korea

The Korean War ostensibly began over an internal disagreement between North and South Korea over how to reunite the peninsula. North Korea wanted to reunite the peninsula under communist governance while South Korea favored a democratic form of governance. Korea presented itself to the rest of the world as a "fault line" between the post Second World War spheres of influence defined by its two parts – the Communist World led by the Soviet Union and the Free World led by the allied powers of the United States, the United Kingdom, and France, with the United States being the new dominant player. Following the invasion of South Korea by the communist North, under the guise of United Nations condemnation, the United States led an effort to push the North Koreans back to the original post-War border roughly at the 38th Parallel. This was to be the limited object of the war. Do not permit the peninsula to come under communist domination. Do not permit communism to advance beyond the current scope of its sphere of influence.

The invasion of the South by the North, along with subsequent brutal treatment of civilians and United States military prisoners fueled the "popular repugnance" of the American people and the Congress to go along with the immediate actions to defend the South and push the North Koreans back across the 38th Parallel. In part due to this popular repugnance, the sudden nature of the involvement in combat, and the sanctioning of actions by the United Nations, apparently neither President Truman nor members of Congress felt compelled to seek a declaration of war. Unwittingly, President Truman and the Congress, with the best of intentions, opened the door to future overreaches in executive power and abdication of essential war powers by the legislative branch. Further their actions in 1950 would set the stage for future abuses by the Congress in trying to right this error in collective judgment.

Korea would seem to fulfill all of Corbett's requirements for a limited war. It is remote from the United States. While it is not an island, it is a narrow peninsula that, to the candid observers back in Washington's war rooms, was definitely in "touch with the sea" and supposedly easily dominated by the U.S. Navy. The Navy of the North would not be capable of threatening the American homeland and of little threat to the United States command of the Korean territorial seas. By brutally invading the South and driving defenders into the sea, the North had provided the "bad behavior" necessary to ignite "popular repugnance" among the American people. By casting the war in terms of good versus evil, freedom versus communism, the President would have an easy time of arousing popular sentiment in support of a new war, especially one so limited in scope compared to what had been concluded less than five short years prior. All that remains of the Corbett limited war test is the strategic isolation of the object, and this, unfortunately, is where the United States failed the test.

Korea cannot be strategically isolated. Even though President Truman insisted upon taking the course of limited war, he failed to take note of the fact that as long as North Korea shared a long border with China, without China's cooperation, limited war against North Korea was and is impossible.

United States forces, under the leadership of General MacArthur, successfully counterattacked the North Korean forces. By achieving the seemingly impossible amphibious landings at Inchon, United Nations forces were able to cut the North's lines of communications and isolate the North Korean Army in the South. United Nations forces were able to then drive the North Koreans northward toward the Yalu River, the border between China and North Korea. By refusing to acknowledge the threat posed by the Red Army massed north of the Yalu; by refusing to attack North Korean stockpiles in Chinese territory; by refusing to believe the Red Army would enter the war on behalf of North Korea; and, by denying United Nations forces the ability to deter the Red Army from crossing the Yalu, President Truman set the table for more than 50 years, and counting, of strategic ambiguity.

On May 27th 2009, North Korea declared that they were no longer bound by the cease fire that began the period of ambiguity. A period of neither victory nor defeat; a period of constant threat; a period of continuous American combat armed presence on the Korean peninsula; and a period that now finds the world threatened by a North Korea ruled by an isolated hereditary monarchy bent on the proliferation of nuclear weapons.

Viet Nam

Viet Nam had been one of the first former colonies of a shrinking European power to fall. Europe, principally France, England, Belgium, Portugal, Holland, Spain and to a lesser extent, Italy and Germany were the main colonial powers that had carved up the world into far flung colonies beginning during the Age of Discovery and reaching an apex during the 19th Century. As the result of changes largely brought about by the outcome of the two world wars, Europe began shedding its less desirable colonies shortly after the Second World War. The shedding of colonies was often haphazard and hasty. With the exception of British colonies, most of the former European colonies were left to fend for themselves. Having no recent tradition of self-governance the former colonies were ripe for the picking by locally grown dictators or Marxist/Leninist dictators sponsored by the Soviet Union. With the emergence in 1949 of China as a communist power, Chinese influence in the Asia/Pacific theatre became a real concern to American presidents.

As stated in his 1961 inaugural address, President Kennedy pledged: "Let every nation know, whether it wishes us well or ill, that we shall pay any price, bear any burden, meet any hardship, support any friend, oppose any foe, in order to assure the survival and the success of liberty." These words provided a framework for military assistance to Viet Nam. President Kennedy had taken up the challenge first put forth by Winston Churchill in his "Iron Curtain Speech" of March 5th 1946 in which he said:

> "The United States stands at this time at the pinnacle of world power. It is a solemn moment for the American democracy. For with this primacy in power is also joined an awe-inspiring accountability to the future. As you look around you, you must feel not only the sense of duty done, but also you must feel anxiety lest you fall below the level of achievement. Opportunity is here now, clear and shining, for both our countries. To reject it or ignore it or fritter it away will bring upon us all the long reproaches of the aftertime.

> It is necessary that constancy of mind, persistency of purpose, and the grand simplicity of decision shall rule and guide the conduct of the English-speaking peoples in peace as they did in war. We must, and I believe we shall, prove ourselves equal to this severe requirement."

He went on to say:
> "I do not believe that Soviet Russia desires war. What they desire is the fruits of war and the indefinite expansion of their power and doctrines."

Beginning with the end of the Second World War; the decent of the "iron curtain" across Europe; the transfer of nuclear weapon technology through espionage to the Soviet Union; the fall of China; the "proxy war" on the Korean peninsula; the tensions of the 1950s; the fall of Cuba in 1958; all served to provide the backdrop of "popular repugnance" among Americans that permitted our involvement in Viet Nam. How hard could it be to provide a poor former French colony with the opportunity to let liberty prosper? By August of 1964 the Tonkin Gulf Incident simply provided the final straw that was necessary for the American people to support the limited object of blocking the advance of communism in Southeast Asia whilst allowing freedom to the people of South Viet Nam.

South Viet Nam, at first glance may appear to provide an appropriate locale for limited war. It does not. While Viet Nam is "remote" and "in touch with the sea", it is neither an island nor a peninsula. Most importantly, it cannot be strategically isolated using naval and air forces alone. South Viet Nam was contiguous with the three other states – Cambodia, Laos and North Viet Nam – making limited war impossible. This fact was apparently lost on President Johnson, Secretary of Defense McNamara, virtually the entire Congress, and senior military officers. With the passage of the Tonkin Gulf Resolution the United States embarked on a limited war with an unlimited objective. Failure was assured from the start.

Starting with the huge increase in ground troop commitment in 1964, President Johnson and his advisors embarked on a strategy largely run from the White House. Perhaps the most prominent element of the war strategy was to avoid Chinese intervention on behalf of the North Vietnamese. They did not want a repeat of the Korean War when U.N. troops pushed too close to the Chinese border and resulted in a Chinese invasion. This meant no ground troops in North Viet Nam. Ground combat was to be limited to the South only. While the United States embarked on an air campaign against military targets in the North, North Viet Nam was still a virtual sanctuary. Even though North Viet Nam lacked a navy of sufficient strength to "command" its territorial sea, the United States essentially handed the North the same benefit of having a navy in limited war – protection of the homeland; thereby giving the North an ability to commit more forces to its ground campaign in South Viet Nam.

In addition to avoiding ground combat in North Viet Nam, the United States also put "off limits," Laos and Cambodia. This strategy left North Viet Nam free reign to transport supplies to its forces and to the Viet Cong using a trail paralleling the South Viet Nam border in Laos to the north and Cambodia to the south. The trail, the Truong Son Road, became known by Americans as the Ho Chi Minh Trail. The Ho Chi

Minh Trail, constructed between 1959 and 1965, consisted of a network of dirt jungle paths and river passages. Along the Trail were a series of underground compartments that housed medical, storage, command, and berthing facilities for the use of the roughly one million men that traversed the Trail during the war. For the decisive period from 1964 to 1968 Cambodia, under the leadership of Prince Sihanouk, observed "neutrality" in the war and turned a blind eye to the Ho Chi Minh Trail and to the network of Viet Cong and North Vietnamese command and control posts within Cambodia's territory. It was not until after the Tet Offensive and U.S. national election of 1968 that the United States attacked sanctuaries within Cambodia. Even then, the primarily air attacks within Cambodia were met with condemnation by members of Congress and by the anti-war movement. In 1973, Congress ordered an end to the bombing of Cambodia against the wishes of President Nixon and his military advisors.

Viet Nam was a confused war. It was supposed to have been a limited war. The ultimate outcome; however, provides us with perhaps the most stark proof of Corbett's theories relative to limited war. It is not enough to simply fulfill "most" of the criteria for limited war. Besides failing the obvious test of not being an island, Viet Nam failed the limited war test on two major levels. (1) The limited object of the United States in the war was not concurrently looked upon as a limited object by North Viet Nam. (2) The inability of the United States to strategically isolate the territorial objective was a fatal flaw in the war strategy.

Kuwait (Persian Gulf War)

On August 2nd 1990 Kuwait, a small desert nation on the northern Persian Gulf, was invaded and taken over by military forces of neighboring Iraq. To Iraq, Kuwait was a limited territorial object that fit the criteria for a limited war. Iraq claimed that Kuwait was responsible for falling oil prices on the world market. Saddam Hussein further justified the taking of Kuwait by claiming that Kuwait was historically a province of Iraq. To the United States and its allies in Europe and in the Persian Gulf region, the invasion was seen as a brazen land-grab that threatened regional stability as well as threatening crude oil supplies. The invasion of Kuwait was roundly condemned by the United Nations Security Council resulting in a flurry of resolutions demanding Iraq's withdrawal and return to preexisting borders and conditions.

The attack coupled with Iraq's refusal to comply with Security Council resolutions provided the necessary "popular repugnance" to consider entering into a limited war to drive Iraq out of Kuwait. Kuwait, while neither an island nor a peninsula, is "in touch with the sea" and could be strategically isolated as it is contiguous with only two other states, Iraq and Saudi Arabia. Since Saudi Arabia was part of a coalition of states condemning Iraq, the only force standing in the way of the limited objective of liberating Kuwait was Iraq itself. Since Iraq's navy was incapable of "commanding the territorial seas" about Kuwait, all criteria for a limited war were met.

On February 23rd 1991 a coalition of military forces led by the United States invaded Iraq and Kuwait with the purpose of driving Iraq's army from Kuwait and to impose upon Iraq new standards of behavior in the region. These limited objectives were attained in four days. Iraq's army was driven from Kuwait and Iraq's government had agreed to conditions outlined in a series of United Nations Security Council resolutions. A limited objective was achieved with a limited contingent of armed forces at a limited cost in terms of "blood and treasure," supposedly a classic case of limited warfare that would make Corbett proud.

Iraq War (Second Persian Gulf War)

Following the cessation of combat on February 27th 1991 and a cease fire agreement under the auspices of the United Nations began a Korea-like period of ambiguity. For more than ten years Iraq consistently violated the terms of its ceasefire. The government of Saddam Hussein remained in total control of the country despite the embarrassment of 1991. In addition to its continued bad behavior, virtually all outside observers believed that Iraq continued to pursue development of weapons of mass destruction. The 1988 use of chemical weapons to kill thousands of Kurdish Iraqis was frequently pointed to as proof of Saddam

Hussein's weapons ambitions. In 1998, partly in criticism of the failure in 1991 to resolve the "Iraq problem," Congress passed, by a vote of 360 to 38 in the House and by unanimous consent in the Senate, the Iraq Liberation Act of 1998 [Appendix II]. This act made it official United States policy to remove Saddam Hussein and to promote a democratic replacement. President Clinton, in signing the act made the following statement:

> "Iraq admitted, among other things, an offensive biological war- fare capability, notably, 5,000 gallons of botulinum, which causes botulism; 2,000 gallons of an- thrax; 25 biological-filled Scud warheads; and 157 aerial bombs. And I might say UNSCOM inspectors believe that Iraq has actually greatly understated its production.... Over the past few months, as [the weapons inspectors] have come closer and closer to rooting out Iraq's remaining nuclear capacity, Saddam has undertaken yet another gam- bit to thwart their ambitions by imposing debilitating con- ditions on the inspectors and declaring key sites which have still not been inspected off limits.... It is obvious that there is an attempt here, based on the whole history of this operation since 1991, to protect whatever remains of his capacity to produce weapons of mass destruction, the missiles to deliver them, and the feed stocks neces- sary to produce them. The UNSCOM inspectors believe that Iraq still has stockpiles of chemical and biological munitions, a small force of Scud-type missiles, and the capacity to restart quickly its production program and build many, many more weapons.... Now, let's imagine the fu- ture. What if he fails to comply and we fail to act, or we take some ambiguous third route, which gives him yet more opportunities to develop this program of weapons of mass destruction and continue to press for the release of the sanctions and continue to ignore the solemn com- mitments that he made? Well, he will conclude that the international community has lost its will. He will then

conclude that he can go right on and do more to rebuild an arsenal of devastating destruction. And some day, some way, I guarantee you he'll use the arsenal."

By October of 2002, Iraq's continued "antagonistic behavior" coupled with the events in New York City a year earlier had caused the sense of "public repugnance" to rise sufficiently to support a limited war in Iraq. By a vote of 297 to 133 in the House and 77 to 23 in the Senate, the Congress passed the Authorization for Use of Military Force Against Iraq Resolution of 2002 [Appendix III]. The resolution was enacted on the 16th of October. The invasion of Iraq commenced on March 20th of 2003 with the limited, yet ambitious, objective of removing Saddam Hussein's regime and promoting a democratic replacement.

Despite the fact that these limited objectives were achieved within roughly two years following the 2003 invasion, in 2009 a large, costly and increasingly unpopular commitment to Iraq remains. In similar fashion to the Viet Nam War, Congressional approval has wavered over time and voices have repeatedly been raised in Congress to remove funding from the effort. Public disapproval has been muted by the fact that the Iraq War has been fought by "someone else's children." The absence of a military draft has removed the major source of discord. The families of the "all volunteer force" have remained steadfastly supportive of the Iraq commitment. Nevertheless, Iraq has been and continues to be a very costly venture in terms of both "blood and treasure." Was Iraq a legitimate object for limited war?

From the standpoint of the United States Iraq appears to have been a limited objective. Following the shock of the September 11th attack in 2001 there was sufficient "popular repugnance" (outrage) to justify entry into a limited war. Where the justification for limited war comes into play is with Iraq itself. While Iraq is certainly remote from the United States and its navy was incapable of defending its own territorial seas, much less threaten the United State home waters, Iraq fails the Corbett test on two major counts: (1) limited object and (2) strategic isolation.

The limited object of creating a democratic government in Iraq seemed to be such a minor concern. The United States government believed that the people of Iraq would welcome American forces as the liberated people of France had welcomed us after the Normandy invasion. The United States government did not comprehend the depth of hatred between Sunni and Shia Muslims within Iraq who put more stock in tribal loyalties than in loyalty to a nation. The United States government miscalculated the number of "foreign fighters" that would resist, to the death, the creation of a democratic form of governance in Iraq. Finally, the power of liberty to overcome systemic corruption with the ancient state of Iraq was grossly overestimated. In other words, we had no idea how much resistance there would be to something we consider to be as natural as breathing – our liberty.

While the failure to understand the vast cultural divide between the United States and Iraq, there is no excuse for the failure to realize that Iraq cannot be strategically isolated and that limited war in Iraq is impossible.

Iraq is neither an island nor a peninsula. It is barely in touch with the sea. In order to strategically isolate Iraq an armed force composed of land, sea and air elements must be able to isolate Iraq from the countries it has its longest borders with – Iran and Syria. Since Iran and Syria have been antagonistic to the limited objective of creating a secular democratic state in the Middle East, both of these states must be strategically isolated in order for the limited objective to be achieved. For the duration of the Iraq War, neither Iran nor Syria has been isolated. Similar to the sanctuary states, Laos and Cambodia, during the Viet Nam War, Iran and Syria have provided sanctuaries for insurgent forces, open borders for foreign fighters to cross, and cross border shipments of weapons and explosives for employment within Iraq. Without the inclusion of Iran and Syria variables in the Iraq equation a lasting solution is virtually impossible to achieve.

Afghanistan

Although our engagement in limited warfare in Afghanistan predates our involvement in Iraq, I have intentionally taken its consideration out of chronologic sequence as our government is now increasing our commitment to operations in Afghanistan as we reduce our commitments in Iraq. President Obama and his allies in the Democrat Party have indicated that Afghanistan is where the true center of conflict is. He has stated that Iraq was a "war of choice" whereas Afghanistan is a war of "necessity." After all, it is somewhere along the Afghanistan/Pakistan border where Osama bin Laden supposedly hides in a mountain cave preparing future attacks on the United States and its allies.

Before analyzing Afghanistan's worthiness for limited war, I would like to summarize Afghanistan's sad historic past in order to put in proper context what our soldiers and marines are being asked to do.

Afghanistan's history can be traced back to roughly 600 B.C. Afghanistan was home to Zoraster, a Persian prophet who lived between 522 and 486 B.C. He founded a monotheistic religion that became known as Zorastrianism. Following the killing of Zoraster, the Persian Empire attempted to absorb Afghanistan with mixed results. The Persian Empire period of Afghan history was characterized by constant tribal revolts against Persian control. This period initiated a tradition that continues to this day.

The first recognizable figure familiar to western educated students that impacted upon Afghanistan was Alexander the Great. Alexander, in a manner of speaking, conquered Afghanistan in 329 B.C. Alexander had a hard time subduing the Afghan people because of their now well-established tradition of constant revolt against central authority. Afghanistan remained under the influence of Alexander's descendants until roughly 50 A.D., when Afghanistan became a major center for the practice of Buddhism and the beginning of Kreshan rule and the Kreshan Empire. The Kreshan period lasted until approximately 220 A.D. when the empire became fragmented.

Afghanistan remained fragmented into tribal centers of varying size until it was invaded by the White Huns in approximately 400 A.D. The White Huns were responsible for the near complete destruction of Buddhist culture within Afghanistan as well as leaving most of the country in ruin. Around 550 A.D., Persia attempted to reassert control over Afghanistan while again being met with the traditional Afghan tribal welcome.

In 652 A.D., Arabs forcibly introduced Islam to Afghanistan. By 962, Afghanistan had become a major center of the Islamic Empire; however, by 1030, the empire began to crumble within Afghanistan due to conflicts among various Muslim leaders. In 1140, Muslim leaders from central Afghanistan moved on and conquered India, thereby exporting the Islamic culture to the Indian subcontinent. Afghanistan's Islamic expansion lasted until 1219, when Afghanistan was invaded by Genghis Khan and his forces. Genghis Kahn inflicted damage on Afghanistan from which it never fully recovered. Among other acts of destruction, Genghis Kahn destroyed advanced irrigation systems. The destruction of irrigation systems resulted in fertile areas being transformed into permanent deserts. The Genghis Kahn invasion and subsequent destruction began a roughly 500-year period of multiple rulers being constantly resisted by Afghans seeking independence, primarily from Persian influence.

In 1747, Afghanistan achieved a form of independence as part of a greater Muslim empire. Unfortunately, this independence was marred by nearly constant state of internal revolt, internal fighting and tribalism. This state of independent upheaval continued until 1836, when Afghanistan was invaded by the British in what would eventually be known as the First Anglo-Afghan War. In this war, the British achieved a limited objective of removing the Afghan leader, Amir Dost Mohammad Khan, and deporting him to exile in India. The British installed a "puppet king," Shah Shuja, in 1839.

As might be expected and in keeping with tradition, Afghans resisted British influence. In one of the most horrific events in the history of the British Empire the main British garrison in Afghanistan was overrun by Afghan resistance fighters in January of 1842. Of the approximate 4,500 British and Indian soldiers and their roughly 12,000 dependent family members and servants living at the garrison, all but one soul was lost in the bloodbath. The annihilation of the British contingent in Afghanistan was followed in April by the assassination of Shah Shuja. By 1843, Afghanistan was independent from outside rule.

While temporarily rid of the British, in 1859 the British, in an apparent strategic isolation move, took Baluchistan, (essentially the entire western half of what is present day Pakistan) and as a result, completely landlocked Afghanistan. For roughly the next twenty years, Afghanistan functioned under several Afghan leaders until being reinvaded by the British in 1878, beginning the Second Anglo-Afghan War.

Despite fierce resistance the British were able to acquire several Afghan territories permanently. Having attained its limited territorial objectives, in 1880 the British allowed Afghanistan to regain some independence, although with considerably reduced territory. Apparently concluding that Afghanistan was an international "basket case," the British also retained the "right" to handle Afghanistan's foreign affairs.

In keeping with the now established practice of abusing Afghanistan, in 1885, Russia attacked and acquired the Panjdeh Oasis in northern Afghanistan. After achieving its limited territorial objective, Russia promised to honor Afghanistan's territorial integrity in the future. A few years later, in 1893, the British formally redrew the Afghan border under the authority of the Durand Treaty. The new border split eastern Afghan tribal areas and annexed them to India. (Today the area is part of Pakistan. The former Afghan tribal territory has never completely accepted the governance of the central Pakistan government. The Durand Line, establishing a border between Afghanistan and Pakistan, has never been recognized by Afghanistan. The Durand Treaty was to have expired in one hundred years. The territory broken off of Afghanistan in 1893 was to have reverted to Afghanistan in 1993 similar to the reversion of Hong Kong to China. Pakistan has poisoned relations with Afghanistan by attempting to get the Taliban to agree to an extension of the Durand Treaty on behalf of Afghanistan).

A few years later, in 1907, the British concluded an agreement with Russia in which Afghanistan was declared outside of Russia's sphere of influence. It presumably placed Afghanistan within Britain's sphere. While Afghanistan played no role in the First World War, while doing some apparent empire "housekeeping," Britain invaded Afghanistan for the third time in 1921 to start the Third, and final, Anglo-Afghan War. For the third time Britain was defeated.

The result of the Third War was Afghanistan regaining control over its own foreign affairs and the beginning of a period of modernization under the leadership of Amanullah Khan. Unfortunately, the period of independence and modernization was short-lived. In 1929 Amanullah

Khan was overthrown. Following a tribal power struggle Nadir Khan became king of Afghanistan. In 1930 Nadir Khan abolished the reforms and modernization measures begun by Amanullah Khan. Nadir was assassinated in 1933 and was replaced as monarch by his son, Zahir. He ruled Afghanistan until 1973.

In 1940, Zahir declared Afghanistan to be neutral during the Second World War. Following the war, breaking with tradition, Britain did not invade Afghanistan for the fourth time. Rather, in 1947, in response to a reinvigorated independence movement within India, Britain began the long, yet relatively peaceful process of dismantling its empire. The Indian colony was divided into two major parts, what would become the Republic of India in 1950 and the Islamic Republic of Pakistan in 1956. Instead of returning the part of Afghanistan that had been taken by the Durand Treaty of 1893, this territory was incorporated into Pakistan, leaving Afghanistan permanently landlocked and territory dominated by ethnic Afghans, within Pakistan. Like other colonies cut loose by other European powers following the Second World War, seeds of future conflicts were sown in the process.

Afghanistan reacted to the partition of India and the creation of Pakistan by formally denouncing the Durand Treaty of 1893 and refused to recognize the boundary between Afghanistan and Pakistan. Afghanistan's protests were largely ignored by the world community. Afghanistan was effectively adrift internationally. As a nonparticipant in the Second World War and as a landlocked mountain state, Afghanistan apparently had little or no strategic value to the West. In response to a 1954 request for military equipment, the United States rebuffed Afghanistan and thereby forfeited an early opportunity to shape Afghanistan's future as an independent state. Afghanistan turned to the Soviet Union for military aid thus establishing a close relationship with the Soviets that would last for the major part of the Cold War period and would negatively influence Afghanistan's internal politics.

In 1965, internal divisions, no doubt encouraged by the Soviet Union, began to arise. With the secret formation of the Afghan Communist Party, the monarchy of Zahir Shah was eventually challenged by communist members of Afghanistan's Parliament. That challenge came in 1973. The monarchy of Zahir Shah was overthrown by a military coup headed by the king's cousin, Daoud Kahn. Zahir, who had been receiving medical treatment in Europe at the time of the coup, was forced into exile. He and his family remained in Italy until his triumphant return, as a private citizen, to Afghanistan in 2002. Daoud Kahn declared himself to be president of the newly established Republic of Afghanistan.

In 1975, Daoud Kahn enacted a new constitution. The new constitution demonstrated that Daoud Kahn wished to reform Afghanistan. Among the elements of the constitution that are frequently pointed to as proof of his reformist intentions, is conferring greater rights upon women. Along with the reforms, however, came a greater desire to solidify his power as president. Daoud Kahn began to purge members of his government who opposed him and his reforms. On April 28th, 1978, Daoud Kahn was assassinated in a coup led by elements of the Afghan Communist Party. With the shift in power to a communist controlled government came mass arrests, torture, and formalized close relations with the Soviet Union. By June, resistance to the communist takeover grew. A descent into near total chaos and anarchy had begun.

1979 was the "year from hell" in Afghanistan. Resistance to the communist government, abetted by clandestine aid from the United States, eventually led to the Soviet invasion of Afghanistan in December. In the words of President Carter's National Security Advisor, Zbigniew Brzezinski, in a memo to the President, "We now have the opportunity to give to the USSR its Vietnam War."

Neither Ian Fleming nor Tom Clancy could make up the events of 1979 in Afghanistan. The mass murders and general lawlessness were punctuated by the kidnap and murder of the U.S. Ambassador, Adolph "Spike" Dubs on the 14th of February. On September 14th, the Soviet backed, Harvard educated economist, communist president, Nur Mohammad Taraki, died of an "undisclosed illness" immediately following a meeting with one of his principal rivals, Hafizullah Amin. Upon the death of Taraki, Amin appointed himself President. Amin was suspected by Taraki's Soviet sponsors of being friendly with the CIA or even being a CIA "plant." Apparently out of concern for Amin's health and welfare, the Soviet's had a specially trained chef flown to Kabul to prepare a "meal" for President Amin. On December 13th Amin, apparently not hungry at the time, gave his food and beverage to his son-in-law, who immediately became very ill. Ironically, he was evacuated to Moscow for medical attention.

On December 24th, in keeping with the 1978 Treaty of Friendship, Cooperation, and Good Neighborliness, signed by President Taraki, Soviet paratroops arrived in Kabul. Having failed in its more "James Bondesque" attempt on Amin's life, on December 27th elements of the KGB and Soviet Special Forces entered the Presidential palace and killed Amin. Shortly after the ensuing Soviet ground invasion, Babrak Karmal, one of the original founders of the Afghan Communist Party was installed as Afghanistan's third president. Thus began the "Soviet Union's Vietnam War."

As was the Afghan "tradition," the invading forces of the Soviet Union and the central communist government met with stiff resistance from a coalition of Muslim guerilla fighters, the Mujahidin. Between December 1979 and February 15th 1989, the Soviet Union deployed more than 100,000 ground troops to Afghanistan. In the end, somewhere between 15,000 and 50,000 Soviet soldiers were killed in action along with more than one million Afghans. Like in prior wars against the British, the tribes of Afghanistan were able to put aside their differences long enough to defeat and drive out their invaders and occupiers. Unfortunately, as in the past, the tribes were unable to unite their country for the good of all Afghans. With the departure of the Soviet troops in 1989 there was a concurrent departure of the various interested parties, like the United States, that had supported the efforts of the Mujahidin. Afghanistan had done the supposedly impossible by going from horrendous to whatever is worse than horrendous. The lost decade of the 80s gave way to the lost decade of the 90s.

After a period of resisting the remnants of the Soviet installed government, the Mujahidin established and Islamic state while continuing border fights with Iranian and Pakistani forces. In 1992 Professor Burhanudin Rabbani, a prominent leader within the Mujahidin, was elected president. By 1994, an Islamic militia, called Taliban (from the Pashto word meaning – teacher), formed and challenged the Rabbani government. In the ensuing fighting between forces loyal to Rabbani and the Taliban, the national capital of Kabul was essentially reduced to rubble. Over the next year, the Taliban consolidated its fundamentalist Islamic hold over much of Afghanistan. Taliban rule was characterized by strict adherence to Islamic Sharia law that is especially oppressive to women.

Internal conflict between the Taliban and those that opposed them would have continued indefinitely were it not for the strong ties forged between the Taliban and another fundamentalist Muslim group, Al Qaeda. Al Qaeda (Arabic for "the base") was formed under the leadership of Saudi-born Osama bin Laden during the latter stages of the Afghan-Soviet War. In 1996, bin Laden and his training operations were evicted from Sudan, around the same time, the Taliban was consolidating its control over Afghanistan. Afghanistan, with the help of the Taliban, became the new home of Al Qaeda. Due to Al Qaeda's attacks against the United States, beginning with the 1993 World Trade Center bombing in New York City, Afghanistan became of renewed interest to the American government of President Clinton. In August of 1998, President Clinton ordered cruise missile attacks on what was believed to be Al Qaeda terrorist training facilities in Afghanistan.

Renewed United States interest in Afghanistan also spelled increased interest from the United Nations. In October of 1999, the Security Council issued Resolution 1267 that sanctioned the Taliban for providing sanctuary for bin Laden and Al Qaeda. When this U.N. sanction failed to achieve the desired result, the Security Council, in December 2000, sanctioned the Taliban for its continued support of terrorism and the cultivation of narcotics. In apparent defiance of the United Nations, in March 2001, the Taliban ordered the systematic destruction of Buddhist antiquities dating from the 5th Century. With the Al Qaeda sponsored attacks on the World Trade Center of September 11th, Afghanistan, Al Qaeda and the Taliban became the focal point of the Global War on Terror. Beginning in October of 2001, United States-led special forces began a "push back" against the Taliban whilst hunting for and attempting to destroy bin Laden and his Al Qaeda facilities in Afghanistan.

By June of 2002, the American led forces had either killed or displaced the Taliban from Afghanistan's major population centers. It is believed that much of the Taliban, along with Osama bin Laden and his Al Qaeda organization, fled eastern Afghanistan for the mountainous former Afghan region in western Pakistan. A transitional government under the leadership of Hamid Karzai was formed. Karzai had gained fame first during the Afghan-Soviet War as an Afghan diplomat and spokesman and later by defying the Taliban's rule. Karzai went on to be elected in 2004 for a five year term as Afghanistan's first democratically elected president.

This is essentially the condition we find ourselves in 2009. The Taliban has reverted to a "traditional" role as insurgent force resisting President Karzai's central government as well as the coalition of American led and dominated NATO forces that continue to fight the Taliban, hunt for Osama bin Laden, and assist in building things like roads, irrigation systems and schools. There is a continued international effort to rid Afghanistan of what was originally millions of landmines laid during the Soviet War. Osama bin Laden, apparently still alive and operating out of somewhere in western Pakistan, is coming under increasing pressure exerted by the Pakistan Army. There is speculation that bin Laden and the Al Qaeda operation may be preparing to relocate to the Horn of Africa. And, despite United Nations condemnation to the contrary, Afghanistan is still the largest producer of heroin in the world.

This short history is meant to provide a context or framework for our intention to fight a limited war in Afghanistan. How does Afghanistan fare with regard to Corbett's test?

First to address the obvious, Afghanistan, while remote from the United States and virtually the rest of the world, has no connection to the sea. It fails this aspect of the Corbett test miserably. Lack of connection with the sea has substantially complicated logistics and air support for combat activities in Afghanistan. Furthermore, Afghanistan is contiguous with countries that are not strategically isolated from the fight, Iran and Pakistan. Iran is openly hostile toward the United States as well as being a proven sponsor of Islamic terrorists. Pakistan's role, on the other hand, is complicated. Even though the limited war effort in Afghanistan would be impossible without Pakistan's cooperation, Pakistan is far from achieving "trusted ally" status. Afghanistan also shares significant borders with the former Soviet republics of Turkmenistan, Uzbekistan, and Tajikistan. These countries though technically independent remain within Russia's sphere of influence. None of the three countries can be considered strategically isolated from Afghanistan. It is hard to imagine a place on earth that is more inappropriate for limited war based on the strategic isolation test.

When the United States initially went into Afghanistan in 2001, the objective was indeed limited. The objective was to attack and kill Osama bin Laden and destroy his Al Qaeda training facilities recently relocated from Sudan to Afghanistan. Afghanistan was picked by bin Laden as a "home" for Al Qaeda operations because of its remoteness, its general state of lawlessness, and because of the Taliban's harmony with bin Laden's goals and methods in bringing about a restoration of an Islamic caliphate. Osama bin Laden also knew that the region between Afghanistan and Pakistan was even more ambiguous in terms of state control than the other regions of the two countries. The region to which Al Qaeda relocated was also geographically conducive to resisting potential military action by a stronger and better armed force. The mountainous topography tipped the war fighting advantage in favor of unconventional guerilla forces familiar with the region through their knowledge of not only the territory but also with the various tribal languages and cultures of the region.

The initial approach by American armed forces was to limit the advantages of the unconventional forces of the Taliban and Al Qaeda through a masterful use of special operations forces. The full history of the operations within Afghanistan by American Special Forces personnel has not yet been written. With knowledge of local languages and customs, even the ability to adapt to local terrain by employing horse transportation in lieu of conventional methods, American Special Forces succeeded in driving the Taliban and Al Qaeda out of the major cities of Afghanistan and into hiding in the mountains along the Afghanistan – Pakistan border. It is unknown whether or not the limited objective of destroying Al Qaeda could have been achieved had the strategic isolation of Afghanistan's eastern region bordering Pakistan been achieved.

Even with strategic isolation, it is most likely a certainty that if the United States had pursued the Taliban and Al Qaeda into the mountains, the resulting heavy losses would have been similar to the losses suffered by the British and Soviets during their ill-fated ventures in prior centuries. The United States would have been fighting on the terms set by the Taliban and by Al Qaeda. In a classic case of a smaller force taking on a larger force, the Afghan fighters could have fought long enough to reach a tipping point at which the cost in terms of blood and treasure would exceed the value of achieving the limited objective. The failure to achieve this limited objective has resulted in roughly seven years of stalemate and seven years of neither victory nor defeat.

In the opinion of the newly elected President of the United States, victory in Afghanistan was not only possible but also was within our grasp were it not for the "distraction" of the "war of choice" in Iraq. One is led to infer from his comments and actions since taking office, that Afghanistan is a just and attainable objective, if not a war of necessity.

Recently, the President has committed the United States to a "date certain" to withdraw combat forces from Iraq. He has also embarked on a strategy to refocus attention on Afghanistan. He has recently appointed a general with a special operations background to lead a "spec ops" centered fight against the Taliban and Al Qaeda along with supervising a renewed push to "train" the Afghans to be self-sufficient militarily; similar to what has been done in Iraq. Efforts to improve Afghanistan's infrastructure and to transform the heroin-trade-based economy will continue as well.

What has Afghanistan done to antagonize the United States and its NATO allies? What is it about Afghanistan that brings about the necessary level of "popular repugnance" among the American people to warrant entering into and then sustaining a successful war effort in Afghanistan? For an answer to these questions, probably the best starting point is the United Nations Security Council Resolutions sanctioning Afghanistan and the Taliban for support of terrorism and for permitting the cultivation of narcotics.

The attacks on the United States homeland of September 11th 2001 are apparently distant in the memory of most Americans. The results of the 2008 general election would seem to validate that assessment. The almost complete lack of attention by the national media to the dramatic drop in casualties in Iraq, along with the ascension of its democratically elected government, reflect the media's "short attention span" and helps to promote a national apathy regarding the progress of the war effort. As the war effort in Afghanistan is reinvigorated, it may be difficult, if not impossible, to reawaken the nation's interest in defeating the Taliban and Al Qaeda.

As the United States commits more troops to the fight in Afghanistan and as the Taliban is more aggressively pursued, the likelihood of greater American casualties is very real. If the general national mood is characterized as apathetic, it is not likely that the American people will have a stomach for a protracted engagement, especially in light of America's experience in Viet Nam and the Soviet Union's experience in Afghanistan.

Judging from Afghanistan's longstanding "tradition" of resisting outside encroachment on its territory, especially in resisting Britain and the Soviet Union, it is highly likely that the "limited object" of permanently deposing the Taliban from the scene is not possible. The United States, going in, will be relatively intolerant of loss in terms of blood and treasure, whilst the Taliban and other tribal groups that rally to their cause, will have a comparatively high tolerance for "pain." The task left to the Taliban is simply to inflict unacceptable casualties on the United States while wearing down the patience of the American people over time.

If there is insufficient popular repugnance against international Islamic terrorism sponsored by the Taliban and Al Qaeda, the threat posed by the Afghan poppy crop is even less likely to raise the hackles of the American people. The "War on Drugs," declared by President Nixon in 1971, is one of the longest and most costly "wars" waged by the United States and there is little hope, or expectation, by the American people that this war will be won any time soon, if ever.

It is true that since 1991, Afghanistan produces more opium than any other country. Ironically, the Taliban banned the cultivation of poppies for opium production upon coming to power. After the Taliban was displaced following the post-September 11th attack on Afghanistan by the United States, with equal irony, opium production reconstituted itself to pre-Taliban levels. Narcotics production is now the principal source of revenue that fuels Islamic terrorism. It is with good reason that the disruption of opium production is viewed by American military strategists as a major, yet limited, objective in Afghanistan. In theory, by eradicating opium production in Afghanistan, Al Qaeda sponsored terrorism can likewise be eradicated.

The cultivation by humans of opium poppies for the purpose of harvesting opium began thousands of years ago. Beginning in the late

1700s, opium poppies were commercially cultivated for worldwide distribution and sale similar to the same commercial cultivation of coffee and tea. Opium was harvested in order to take advantage of the morphine, opium's principal euphoria-inducing and pain-relieving component, while tea and coffee was harvested in order to take advantage of the stimulant caffeine. Opium was used by the British as part of a triangle trade with China. The side benefit to the British was that creating a dependence on opium in China allowed Britain to greatly control and manipulate the Chinese to Britain's advantage. For the entirety of the 19th Century, opium enjoyed worldwide commercial distribution, use, and social acceptance similar to that of tea and coffee.

In the 1890s, a chemical process was invented that resulted in what was commercially advertised as "a heroine in the war on pain." The product of this invention came to be known as heroin. Heroin is a synthetic derivative of morphine. Production of heroin involves the processing of opium with acid, followed by the application of a neutralizing agent such as ammonia. In the late 1800s, heroin was believed to be a safer alternative to morphine and its often nasty side effects.

By the late 1890s, the addictive qualities and non-medicinal "recreational" use of heroin was better understood. A Protestant church-inspired movement arose in Britain and the United States that challenged the continued commercial availability of opiates. The anti-opium movement was swept along through its close alliance with the larger temperance movement seeking to eradicate alcohol consumption. By 1914, the United States Congress had passed the Harrison Narcotics Act that imposed, for the first time, restrictions on what Americans could do with their bodies. A few years later, the League of Nations adopted restrictions on the recreational use of heroin and other derivatives of opium. Unfortunately, the "genie was already out of the bottle," the "horse was already out of the barn." The result of international restrictions of the production and use of heroin had the unintended consequence of creating a businessman's dream – insatiable demand and limited supply. Even better for a heroin-trafficking businessman – an outlawed, untaxed, substance with insatiable demand and limited supply – an opportunity for huge profits with none of those pesky taxes like those on alcohol or tobacco products.

Heroin demand throughout the world remained constant throughout the 20th Century. Large-scale opium poppy cultivation migrated from India to the Golden Triangle of Southeast Asia. The Triangle that included parts of Burma, Thailand, Laos and Viet Nam became the primary source of opium for heroin production by the 1950s. By the 1970s, fueled by a huge increase of heroin use within the United States, the principal source of opium for heroin production moved to the Golden Crescent made up of regions within Iran, Pakistan and Afghanistan. While heroin demand worldwide has fluctuated somewhat since the 1970s, by 2009, it is experiencing resurgence in popularity, especially among young adults in the United States. The principal source of heroin being used in the United States comes from Columbia and to a lesser extent, Mexico.

According to a United States State Department 2007 report, Afghanistan not only remains a major cultivator of opium poppies, it currently produces roughly 90 percent of the world's heroin. The rise to prominence as the world's preeminent heroin producer has come about since the fall of the Taliban and the occupation of Afghanistan by United States and NATO armed forces. The expansion in heroin production has been facilitated by the improvement in Afghanistan's road transportation infrastructure. Apparently, the majority of the chemicals required to extract heroin from opium are transported by tank trucks crossing the northern border of Afghanistan. It appears that chemicals for heroin production are coming through unabated from the former Soviet republics. Once the heroin is processed in one of the multiple heroin factories within Afghanistan, it is transported by modern means (not on the backs of donkeys) over a route tantamount to a new "Spice Road of the 21st Century." From points believed to be in the Balkans, perhaps Kosovo, the heroin is distributed by criminal networks, including the Mafia.

Up to this point in the American and NATO involvement in Afghanistan, the strategy with regard to opium cultivation and heroin production has been to eradicate individual poppy fields; those picturesque landscapes flanked by jagged mountains and tended by ruddy-faced old men going about the painstaking process of lancing each poppy pod before scraping away the putty-like opium sap. While apparently aware of the locations of the at least 25 heroin factories, it has not been the policy of the coalition to interrupt the production of heroin or interfere with the transport of the heroin to its worldwide illicit market. Of course, this strategy makes about as much sense as cutting off a hangnail in order to treat lung cancer.

Perhaps it is not the intent of the American government and its NATO partners to disrupt the major source of the world's heroin. Maybe the intent is to merely give the "impression" that we are trying to interrupt heroin production through carefully staged photo ops. If this is the case, then this limited objective is not worth one drop of American blood or one penny of American treasure. The heroin trade is largely a creation of the west, especially Britain. It is largely the west's insatiable appetite for heroin that has created and sustained the high demand for illicit opiates. Rather than approaching this objective, which I would contend is nearly without limit, from the "supply side," perhaps it is incumbent on the United States and its NATO allies to search for a new approach from the "demand side."

Clearly, when put to Corbett's test for limited war, Afghanistan fails on multiple levels. When the results of Corbett's test are combined with the lessons learned by the British in their three wars and the Soviets in their one, Afghanistan becomes even less worthy of consideration for limited warfare.

War Powers

As previously mentioned, Viet Nam was not a declared war; it was an "authorized" war by way of the Tonkin Gulf Resolution of 1964 [Appendix II]. This resolution began a trend that lasts to this day. In 1973, in the tumultuous period of Watergate, an adversarial Congress passed, over President Nixon's veto, the War Powers Resolution [Appendix III]. This resolution formalized what the Tonkin Gulf Resolution started, greater Congressional control of the heretofore executive power of Commander in Chief of the armed forces.

In his dissenting opinion of the landmark Roe v. Wade Supreme Court case of the same year, 1973, Associate Justice William Rehnquist made a comment that could well apply to the War Powers Resolution. The Court had discovered a right to privacy, hence a right of women to have abortions, existed in the due process clause of the 14th Amendment. Rehnquist argued that had the drafters of the 14th Amendment, (a Civil War amendment ratified in 1868) intended to include the right to an abortion in this amendment to the Constitution, they would have. By 1868 there were 36 state or territorial laws limiting abortion. Rehnquist wrote:

> There apparently was no question concerning the validity of this provision or of any of the other state statutes when the Fourteenth Amendment was adopted. The only conclusion possible from this history is that the drafters did not intend to have the Fourteenth Amendment withdraw from the States the power to legislate with respect to this matter.

One could make an even stronger argument to the War Powers Resolution. In 1973, Congress rationalized its right to regulate the executive's war powers through the novel new application of the clause in Article I, Section 8 of the Constitution that states:

81

The Congress shall have Power –

To make all Laws which shall be necessary and proper for carrying into Execution the foregoing Powers, and all other Powers vested by this Constitution in the Government of the United States, or in any Department or Officer thereof.

If the drafters of the Constitution understood one matter better than all others, it was the matter of national security and the war powers of the Legislative and Executive branches of the national government. Had the drafters intended the Congress to use the "necessary and proper" clause of Article I for the purpose of regulating the war powers of the Executive branch, they would have enumerated that power specifically. Section 8 of Article I [Appendix I], being the enumerated powers of the Congress, in fact includes deliberate and specific powers of Congress relative to fighting of wars and the administration of the armed forces. Among those enumerated powers the following specifically deal with war and the armed forces:

The Congress shall have Power –

To declare War, grant Letters of Marque and Reprisal, and make Rules concerning Captures on Land and Water;

To raise and support Armies, but no Appropriation of Money to that Use shall be for a longer Term than two Years;

To provide and maintain a Navy;

To make Rules for Government and Regulation of the land and naval Forces;

To provide for calling forth the Militia to execute the Laws of the Union, suppress Insurrections and repel Invasions;

To provide for organizing, arming, and disciplining, the Militia, and for governing such Part of them as may be employed in the Service of the United States, reserving to the States respectively, the Appointment of the Officers, and the Authority of training the Militia according to the discipline prescribed by Congress

To exercise exclusive Legislation in all Cases whatsoever, over... all Places purchased by the Consent of the Legislature of the State in which the Same shall be, for the Erection of Forts, Magazines, Arsenals, dock-yards and other needful buildings.

The drafters of the Constitution understood the sheer folly of waging war by committee. In painstaking detail and astounding literacy, Alexander Hamilton explains the intentions the drafters of the Constitution had for the Executive in Federalist Papers Numbers 67 through 77. Specifically, with regard to the war powers of the Executive, in expanding upon Section 2 of Article II he stated in the first paragraph of Federalist Number 74:

The President of the United States is to be "commander-in-chief of the army and navy of the United States and of the militia of the several States when called into the actual service of the United States." The propriety of this provision is so evident in itself and it is at the same time so consonant to the precedents of the State constitutions in general, that little need be said to explain or enforce it. Even those of them which have in other respects coupled the Chief Magistrate with a council have for the most part concentrated the military authority in him alone. Of all the cares or concerns of government, the direction of war most peculiarly demands those qualities which distinguish the exercise of power by a single hand. The direction of war implies the direction of the common strength; and the power of directing and employing the common strength forms a usual and essential part in the definition of the executive authority.

The Congress of 1973 that defied the intentions of the Constitution's drafters were either ignorant of the conditions of the American Revolution and the experience of the thirteen original states that spawned the words of Hamilton, or, they were blinded by their own partisan political ambitions and animosities toward the President. Regardless, this power grab by Congress has severely hampered the ability of the United States to effectively wage war.

The Tonkin Gulf Resolution established the use of "wiggle words" that enabled Congress to float with the vagaries of changing public opinion rather than making and holding to difficult decisions. Words that enabled the Congress to stand in the cheering section on the stage behind the President during the initial decision-making phase of whether or not to go to war, yet words that permitted the same cheering section to skulk off the same stage through a hidden trapdoor, leaving the President under the hot klieg lights of public opinion, alone.

In the resolution, Congress appears to act boldly in providing the President authority "to take all necessary steps, including the use of armed force;" while at the same time providing themselves the ability to say later to the President that he should have used non-military means. The resolution is concluded with the following paragraph:

> Sec 3. This resolution shall expire when the President shall determine that the peace and security of the area is reasonably assured by international conditions created by action of the United Nations or otherwise, except that it may be terminated earlier by concurrent resolution of the Congress.

This final section provides Congress with the ultimate trap door. Regardless of what the President says or does; regardless of what the United Nations may say or do; the Congress reserves the right to terminate use of the armed forces of the United States by a simple vote. This is a direct departure from the sole power given to the Congress to influence the employment of the armed forces through the appropriations process.

The War Powers Resolution expanded on the wiggle words and the trap doors. After gathering additional war powers unto itself by way of the "necessary and proper" clause, Congress goes on to separating the use of armed forces into three distinct categories. Section 2(c) states:

> The constitutional powers of the President as Commander-in-Chief to introduce United States Armed Forces intohostilities, or into situations where imminent involvement in hostilities is clearly indicated by the circumstances, are exercised only pursuant to (1) a declaration of war, (2) specific statutory authorization, or (3) a national emergency created by attack upon the United States, its territories or possessions, or its armed forces.

While acknowledging the existence of the Constitutional "declared war," Congress created two categories of armed conflict that exist outside of the Constitution. These two new categories, those arising out of "statutory authorization" or out of "national emergency," are subject to Congressional oversight not envisioned by the drafters of the Constitution. Clearly, Congress prefers the categories it has created over the Constitutional "declared" variety of armed conflict. Congress recognized that while the Constitution provides for consultation with the Congress, culminating in a declaration of war, it also recognized that aside from the appropriations process, that is where consultation ended and the war powers of the Commander-in-Chief took over.

Congress in Section 4(a) of the Resolution effectively admits that there is a major distinction between "declared war" and their "statutorily authorized war". 4(a) begins by saying:

> In the absence of a declaration of war, in any case
> in which United States Armed Forces are introduced –

What should we infer from this distinction?

Congress understands that a declaration of war under their war powers from Article I Section 8 is tantamount to a sacred pledge to commit Congressional support for the duration of the war being declared. A word of honor that the most partisan politician would feel duty bound to uphold.

On the other hand, the statutorily authorized war provides Congress with a trap door to sneak out of in the event the war becomes costly or loses the enthusiastic support of the people. Statutory authorization can be obtained with the same level of commitment and enthusiasm required by a Congressional resolution declaring April 2009, Jazz Appreciation Month – none.

The adoption of the War Power Resolution of 1973 has allowed Congress to assume part of the Presidential power of Commander-in-Chief of the armed forces while avoiding the accountability for the actions and decisions of the Commander-in-Chief put on the President alone. Members of Congress can vacillate and equivocate with impunity.

The events of the lead-up to the Second Iraq War are instructive. Shortly after the dust had settled and the Iraqi Army had limped back to their barracks following the four days of Operation Desert Storm on February 28th, 1991, Iraq began violating the terms spelled out in United Nations Security Council Resolutions 686 and 687. Over the next roughly seven years, Iraq, under the continued leadership of dictator, Saddam Hussein, systematically challenged the authority of the United Nations. The work of the United Nations Special Commission on Iraq (UNSCOM) had been repeatedly hampered in its attempts to account for Iraq's weapons of mass destruction. After repeated attempts by United Nations Secretary General, Kofi Annan, to coax and cajole Saddam Hussein into compliance with Iraq's obligations, the United Nations Security Council issued Resolution 1154. 1154, adopted on March 2nd 1998, warned that any further violations of the agreements reached between Mr. Annan and Saddam Hussein would be met with the "severest consequences." This resolution supposedly meant that after seven years, there would be "no more fooling around" by Iraq and "no more Mr. Nice Guy" by the United Nations.

Around this same time key Clinton Administration officials made strong public statements critical of Iraq. National Security Adviser, Sandy Berger stated:

"Saddam will rebuild his arsenal of weapons of mass destruction and some day, some way, I am certain he will use that arsenal again, as he has 10 times since 1983."

86

Secretary of State, Madeline Albright claimed that:

"Saddam's goal is to achieve the lifting of U.N. sanctions while retaining and enhancing Iraq's weapons of mass destruction programs. We cannot, we must not and we will not let him succeed."

Apparently taking a cue from the United Nations the United States and members of President Clinton's administration, Congress went about chronicling Iraq's transgressions between February 1991 and the summer of 1998. Public Law 105-235, a Joint Resolution entitled Iraqi Breach of International Obligations [Appendix IV], resulted. In true War Powers Resolution "wiggle word" "trap door" style, Congress forwarded the following to President Clinton for his signature and action:

Resolved by the Senate and House of Representatives of the United States of America in Congress assembled, That the Government of Iraq is in material and unacceptable breach of its international obligations, and therefore the President is urged to take appropriate action, in accordance with the Constitution and relevant laws of the United States, to bring Iraq into compliance with its international obligations.

The Resolution was passed by a 407 to 6 vote in the House of Representatives and the Senate passed the measure by unanimous consent, meaning, no senator objected to the resolution.

President Clinton said at the time:

"The community of nations may see more and more of the very kind of threat Iraq poses now: a rogue state with weapons of mass destruction, ready to use them or provide them to terrorists. If we fail to respond today, Saddam and all those who would follow in his footsteps will be emboldened tomorrow."

August 1998 was a momentous month. American embassies in Kenya and Tanzania were bombed by a group also associated with previous bombing attacks on United States interests – the World Trade Centerbombing of 1993 and the Khobar Towers bombing of 1996. The group was Al Qaeda. On the 20th of August, President Clinton ordered the first shots of the War on Terror by authorizing the cruise-missile attacks on purported Al Qaeda chemical weapon factory in Sudan and training facilities in Afghanistan.

After taking their usual August summer vacation Congress returned to Washington and continued micro-management of the President's options regarding Iraq. In a letter signed by a number of senators, including John Kerry of my home state of Massachusetts stated:

> "We urge you, after consulting with Congress, and consistent with the U.S. Constitution and laws, to take necessary actions (including, if appropriate, air and missile strikes on suspect Iraqi sites) to respond effectively to the threat posed by Iraq's refusal to end its weapons of mass destruction programs."

By the end of October 1998 Congress had approved another measure under Public Law 105-338, Iraq Liberation Act of 1998. In its best "having its cake and eating it too" style:

> ...the Congress urges the President to call upon the United Nations to establish an international criminal tribunal for the purpose of indicting, prosecuting, and imprisoning Saddam Hussein and other Iraqi officials who are responsible for crimes against humanity, genocide, and other criminal violations of international law.

Congress went on to say:

> It is the sense of the Congress that once the Saddam Hussein regime is removed from power in Iraq, the United States should support Iraq's transition to democracy by

providing immediate and substantial humanitarian assistance to the Iraqi people, by providing democracy transition assistance to Iraqi parties and movements with democratic goals, and by convening Iraq's foreign creditors to develop a multilateral response to Iraq's foreign debt incurred by Saddam Hussein's regime.

Congress, after presenting an objective that could not possibly be attained without the employment of military force, concludes by saying:

Nothing in this Act shall be construed to authorize or otherwise speak to the use of United States Armed Forces (except as pro-vided in section 4(a) (2)) in carrying out this Act.

[Note: Section 4(a)(2) permitted military assistance to Iraqi democratic opposition organizations in the form of "... the drawdown of defense articles from the stocks of the Department of Defense, defense services of the Department of Defense, and military education and training for such organizations."]

This resolution was passed by the House of Representatives in a 360 to 38 vote and again by unanimous consent in the Senate. The Congress was exercising its power, self-granted by the War Powers Resolution of 1973. Congress was urging on the one hand the President to use his power as Commander-in-Chief of the Armed Forces while on the other hand reminding the President that he may not use his power as Commander-in-Chief unless first authorized by Congress.

Interlaced with the events of the late summer and fall of 1998 was the matter that came to be known as the Lewinsky Affair. The President's actions during the ensuing investigation into his personal behavior were further complicated by the movie, *Wag the Dog*, released a year earlier, in which the public is distracted from a fictitious president's sex scandal by a contrived war. On the eve of his impeachment, the 16th of December, President Clinton ordered an air assault on military targets in Iraq. The air campaign lasted four days and had the stated purpose, in the words of President Clinton in his December 16th address to the nation:

> "They are designed to degrade Saddam's capacity
> to develop and deliver weapons of mass destruction, and
> to degrade his ability to threaten his neighbors."

The limited object of "degrading" Iraq's "capacity" and "ability" resolved nothing nor did the earlier attacks on Al Qaeda. The air and missile attacks had succeeded in placing the Iraq/Al Qaeda dilemma on "simmer" for the next three years. The next time that the Congress would dust off the War Powers Resolution would come in 2002 following the "boil over" of September 11th 2001. Congress would revisit the Iraq problem.

In October of 2002 Congress employed the same format and language employed in the 1998 Iraqi Breach of International Obligations Joint Resolution when they authored Public Law 107-243, Authorization for Use of Military Force Against Iraq Resolution [Appendix V]. The international and national landscape had changed somewhat since the 1998 resolutions against Iraq. While little had changed with regard to Saddam Hussein's behavior the United States had sustained the September 11th attacks; had pursued Al Qaeda terrorists in Afghanistan; and, had undergone a shift in political party in the White House through the very close and ultimately contentious election of 2000.

The discussion that preceded the October vote included much of the same rhetoric that accompanied the 1998 votes condemning Iraq and warning of the threat Saddam Hussein posed to international stability. The two senators from Massachusetts were, through seniority and experience, in the middle of the discussion. Senator Kerry stated that:

> "I will be voting to give the president of the United States the authority to use force – if necessary – to disarm Saddam Hussein because I believe that a deadly arsenal of weapons of mass destruction in his hands is a real and grave threat to our security."

On September 27[th,] Massachusetts' senior senator, Edward Kennedy stated that:

"There is no doubt that Saddam Hussein's regime is a serious danger, that he is a tyrant, and that his pursuit of lethal weapons of mass destruction cannot be tolerated. He must be disarmed."

A few days later, Senator Kennedy would vote against the resolution.

The joint resolution to authorize the use of military force in Iraq ultimately passed with greater than two-thirds majorities in both houses. The House passed the resolution by a vote of 296 to 133. The Senate, unlike the earlier unanimous votes that urged President Clinton to take "appropriate action" against Iraq, passed the measure by a vote of 77 to 23. With the exception Rhode Island's Lincoln Chafee, the vote in the Senate was along party lines. What had changed? Why had 23 senators passed up the opportunity to declare war? Why had the ultimate governmental decision to - use military force against an enemy - been reduced to just another political act in the eyes of so many senators? Were the senators hedging their bets so that if a war in Iraq became unpopular, as Viet Nam had in the late 60s, they would have a political advantage in future elections?

In the fall of 2002 and winter of 2003, President Bush had the strong support of the Congress and of American public opinion to take military action in Iraq. Couched in the language of the War Powers Resolution, the Authorization to Use Military Force employed the same "wiggle words" and "trap doors" in a framework that appeared to be supportive and strong. Congress assured that while it reserved the right to oversee and micro-manage the use of military force, it also assured that in the event of difficulties or failure it would be the president that would be fully accountable. The resolution stated that:

The President is authorized to use the Armed Forces of the United States as he determines to be necessary and appropriate in order to —

(1) Defend the national security of the United States against the continuing threat posed by Iraq; and

(2) Enforce all relevant United Nations Security Council
    resolutions regarding Iraq.

By promoting a "war by committee" approach to managing a war rather than leading it, the Congress provided its members a "trap door"by which they could escape at a later date. Congress left to the individual opinions of its members to determine if the president's decisions were "necessary and appropriate." In effect, Congress had provided the nation with 535 "Monday morning quarterbacks" for directing the application of military force – a recipe for disaster. Congress had successfully "thread the needle" of being able to "statutorily authorize" in strong terms while doing so with less than full resolve. Congress would commit young men and women to combat while preserving its member's political options in the future.

The months immediately following the passage of the Joint Resolution on October 16th, 2002 were characterized by debate within the international community as well as within the Bush Administration as to how to proceed. Even after more than a decade of repeated violations of United Nations sanctions and Security Council resolutions, there were some that favored continued attempts for a diplomatic solution. Within the Administration there was an active debate as to the proper military strategy to follow and the number of troops necessary to carry out a ground campaign against Iraq. Unfortunately for President Bush he could not choose all proposed solutions. Ultimately he had to decide between continued diplomacy after more than ten years of failure, or, military action. He chose military action. He then had to decide which professional advice to take and which not to with regard to the military strategy. This after all was a "limited war" to be fought with a "limited contingent" of force. He had to decide what that limited contingent would be. Some favored overwhelming numbers while others favored greater "finesse" in the employment of military force. He ended up choosing finesse over sheer numbers, numbers that the United States no longer had following the "Peace Dividend" years of the 90s.

President Bush's decision making process was bolstered in late 2002 and early 2003 by many members of Congress, even some that did not vote for the October Resolution. Senator John Edwards of North

Carolina in remarks made on October 10th, 2002 said:

> "Saddam Hussein's regime represents a grave threat to America and our allies, including our vital ally, Israel. For more than two decades, Saddam Hussein has sought weapons of mass destruction through every available means. We know that he has chemical and biological weapons. He has already used them against his neighbors and his own people, and is trying to build more. We know that he is doing everything he can to build nuclear weapons, and we know that each day he gets closer to achieving that goal.
>
> The debate over Iraq is not about politics. It is about national security. It should be clear that our national security requires Congress to send a clear message to Iraq and the world: America is united in its determination to eliminate forever the threat of Iraq's weapons of mass destruction."

Three months later Senator John Kerry of Massachusetts, consistent with previous statements, again expressed his support of action in Iraq by stating on January 23rd, 2003:

> "We need to disarm Saddam Hussein. He is a brutal, murderous dictator, leading an oppressive regime. We all know the litany of his offenses. He presents a particularly grievous threat because he is so consistently prone to miscalculation....And now he is miscalculating America's response to his continued deceit and his consistent grasp for weapons of mass destruction. That is why the world, through the United Nations Security Council, has spoken with one voice, demanding that Iraq disclose its weapons programs and disarm. So the threat of Saddam Hussein with weapons of mass destruction is real, but it is not new. It has been with us since the end of the Persian Gulf War."

All the threats of the previous 11 years; all the United Nations resolutions; all the ideas and advice, came down to one fateful decision. In the early morning hours of March 20th, 2003 a large coalition force invaded Iraq with the expressed purpose of defeating the Iraqi Army and deposing Saddam Hussein and his regime. In accordance with the Iraq Liberation Act of 1998, democracy was to be fostered by the United States in Iraq. The objectives of defeating the army and deposing the government were achieved by the 30th of April. By the end of 2003 Saddam Hussein was in custody and his sons, apparent heirs to Saddam's dictatorship, were dead. According to public opinion surveys, compiled by the Pew Research Center, indicate that a majority of Americans (71 percent) felt that going to war in Iraq was the "right decision." An even larger number (90 percent) felt the war was going "very/fairly well." The public approval numbers remained above fifty percent for the remainder of 2003.

The initial push into Iraq was enthusiastically covered by the news media. Trying to avoid any and all real or perceived pitfalls in press relations during the Viet Nam War, the American military offered unprecedented access to the war from the first moments of the invasion. "Imbedded" news personalities were accorded celebrity status as they rode into Iraq atop military vehicles. Images and accounts of the assault were available to the American people frequently in real time on a near "24/7" basis. Following the fall of Baghdad and other major Iraqi cities, the attention span of the media celebs, and with them the American people, began to wane. Even though the war continued on at a different pace, now with different, less spectacular objectives, the news media and a growing number of the American people were ready to "move on."

To the surprise of many, including military officers who had apparently never learned from Clausewitz that war is a reciprocal activity, the aftermath of the invasion did not go as smoothly as some had predicted (hoped). The Iraqi Army and members of Saddam Hussein's regime had evidently read the chapter in Vom Krieg that dealt with fighting against and wearing down a stronger force with a weaker force. They understood the impact that hit-and-run weapons would have on public opinion in the United States. They understood the frustration caused by random and brutal killing inflicted by Improvised Explosive Devises (IEDs). They understood that the underpinning foundation of the American people could be eroded by a fight that appeared to be without purpose and without end. They may also have understood that a predominantly Christian nation like the United States would have no frame of reference in understanding the brutality wreaked on Muslims by Muslims. "Sunni" and "Shiite" became new words in the American vocabulary.

It is hard to say when public opinion on the Iraq War began to sour. Not a single event, not a single time period can be pointed to. I suspect, like in many things, it was a combination of events and loss of attention over time. The news media elites had gone home early, leaving the reporting to younger correspondents trying to make names for themselves as their "forefathers" had in Viet Nam. War reporting was heavily influenced by the Viet Nam template. So too, was the Democratic Party's nascent presidential campaign. The campaign became the "next story" for the press and the people.

By the summer of 2003, the news story was of the surprising rise in popularity of Howard Dean, former governor of Vermont. Governor Dean shocked the Democratic Party and the media by doing better than any of the other early candidates by excelling in the chief measure of popularity – how much money had been raised. Dean was the first to tap into the money-raising potential of the Internet. By the early summer of 2003, Dean had raised a huge amount of money through small donations over the Internet. He successfully tapped into a major portion of the party's far left and anti-war base. Aside from his lead in raising money, Governor Dean had successfully given voice to the heretofore unfocussed anti-war movement. It was time to dust off those Country Joe and the Fish records.

Howard Dean's campaign, although ultimately unsuccessful in primaries, succeeded in making the Iraq War a dominant issue of the 2004 campaign. Candidates who had recently voiced their support for removing Saddam Hussein, changed their tunes to better conform to perceived changes in public opinion. They recognized that the primary voters would be dominated by the left-leaning anti-war contingent within the Democrat Party. They recognized that the ultimate nomination would be largely determined by the candidate's position on the war. They began heading for the "trap door" provided to them by the War Powers Resolution and its "offspring," the Authorization for use of Military Force against Iraq Resolution of 2002.

Senator John Forbes Kerry, (Democrat – Massachusetts) ultimately became the Democratic Party's nominee for president in 2004. His words and actions perhaps best serve to illustrate my points about the War Powers Resolution.

In the 2004 presidential campaign Senator Kerry presented himself as a proud veteran of the Viet Nam War. He was a self-professed expert on matters of international relations and war. At the 2004 Democratic National Convention, held in Boston, Kerry spotlighted his military service by having himself introduced by former Georgia U.S. Senator Max Cleland and flanked by many of his crewmen from his Viet Nam experience as commanding officer of what was known as a Swift Boat. Following a military salute to the audience, Kerry's first words upon being introduced were: "I'm John Kerry, and I'm reporting for duty."

Many of us who also served in the military and specifically in the Navy, listening that night were a bit taken aback by this show of patriotic fervor and ardor for the military. We remembered John Kerry's rise to prominence a bit differently than what was being portrayed at the Convention. Senator Kerry first became known to me shortly after I got out of Navy boot camp and was attending a Navy school in San Diego to qualify me as an Interior Communications Electrician.

It was in April 1971 and a recently discharged Viet Nam Vet from Massachusetts was testifying before the Senate Foreign Relations Committee. He was representing one of the many anti-war groups of the time called Vietnam Veterans Against the War (VVAW). I remember asking myself at the time "What is he running for?" I, like most Americans, that heard his words that day were shocked by his testimony. For those of us in uniform at the time his words regarding what he called the "Winter Soldier Investigation" were the most troubling. Among the most volatile of his charges had to do with what he alleged to be widespread misconduct of American servicemen in Viet Nam. In referring to a recent convention of supposed Viet Nam veterans in Detroit he said:

"They told the stories at times they had person-ally raped, cut off ears, cut off heads, taped wires from portable telephones to human genitals and turned up the power, cut off limbs, blown up bodies, randomly shot at civilians, razed villages in fashion reminiscent of Genghis Khan, shot cattle and dogs for fun, poisoned food stocks, and generally ravaged the countryside of South Vietnam in addition to the normal ravage of war, and the normal and very particular ravaging which is done by the applied bombing power of this country."

Although the Winter Soldiers Investigation was later completely discredited, John Kerry's words lit the torch of hatred for American ser-vicemen by Americans for the next decade or more. Those of us in the service during the 1970s, drew a straight line from the way we were treated to John Kerry's words on that day in April 1971.

I had been correct to be skeptical of John Kerry's motivation for having served in the Navy and then taking on a prominent leadership role in the VVAW – he was indeed running for something. In the next year John Kerry moved from Worcester, Massachusetts to Lowell so that he could challenge a Republican U.S. Representative. This got my atten-tion again since my hometown is a suburb of Lowell. John Kerry was about the only Democrat to not get elected that year in Massachusetts riding the coattails of presidential candidate George McGovern, (quite a distinction considering that McGovern carried only the Commonwealth of Massachusetts and the District of Columbia that year).

John Kerry remained politically active in Massachusetts while he attended law school after his defeat in the 1972 election. Following graduation from law school in 1976, he became a prosecutor in the Middlesex County District Attorney's office. He remained as an assis-tant district attorney before doing a brief stint in private law practice until the next opportunity for elective office presented itself. In 1982, he was elected Lieutenant Governor to Michael Dukakis. Lieutenant Gov-ernor, along with residency in Lowell, provided the springboard needed to get into the U.S. Senate. In 1984, Lowell resident, Senator Paul Tsongas announced that he was stepping down due to health concerns. John Kerry became the junior senator from Massachusetts following the 1984 election.

Senator Kerry's opportunity to exercise his military and international expertise came in 1990 following the August invasion of Kuwait by Iraq. It would seem that the lead-up to Operation Desert Storm by a coalition of U.N. members states led by the United States, coupled with the strong words of United Nations Security Council Resolution 678, along with eleven other U.N. resolutions, would provide the justification necessary to achieve a strong, bipartisan, if not unanimous, approval from Congress to authorize the use of military force.

By early January 1991, five months and 12 United Nations Security Council resolutions later, Congress was ready to act. In a resolution[102-1] authored by the Chairman of the Senate Armed Services Committee, Sam Nunn of Georgia and co-sponsored by many other senators of his party, including John Kerry, the Senate proposed the following:

> That:
> (a) The Congress is firmly committed to reversing Iraq's brutal and illegal occupation of Kuwait.
> (b) The Congress authorizes the use of American military force to enforce the United Nations economic embargo against Iraq; to defend Saudi Arabia from direct Iraqi attack; and to protect American forces in the region.
> (c) The Congress believes that continued application of international sanctions and diplomatic efforts to pressure Iraq to leave Kuwait is the wisest course at this time and should be sustained, but does not rule out declaring war or authorizing the use of force at a later time should that be necessary to achieve the goal of forcing Iraqi troops from Kuwait.
> (d) The Congress pledges its full and continued support for sustaining the policy of increasing economic and diplomatic pressure against Iraq; for maintaining our military options; and for efforts to increase the mili-

tary and financial contributions made by allied nations.

(e) The Constitution of the United States vests all power to declare war in the Congress of the United States. Congress will expeditiously consider any future Presidential request for a declaration of war or for authority to use military force against Iraq, in accordance with the following procedures:

The resolution failed on a near party-line vote of 46 "yes" to 53 "no" votes. All "yes" votes, including Mr. Kerry's, were Democrats while all the Republicans were joined by ten Democrats in voting down the resolution. It is interesting to note that the legislation strongly invokes the Constitution and the power of Congress to "declare war" in accordance with its enumerated powers, a measure that would considerably hamper the ability of Congress to dictate the terms of the use of military force in accordance with the War Powers Resolution of 1973.

Soon after the defeat of Resolution 102-1[Joint Resolution Regarding United States policy to reverse Iraq's occupation of Kuwait], Resolution 102-2 [Joint Resolution To authorize the use of United States Armed Forces pursuant to United Nations Security Council Resolution 678] was offered as a counter proposal. This resolution differed from the earlier defeated measure in that it skipped the phase of continued use of sanctions and diplomacy, favored by Senator Kerry, and immediately authorized the President to employ military force in accordance with the War Powers Resolution of 1973. The resolution stated:

This joint resolution may be cited as the Authorization for Use of Military Force Against Iraq Resolution:

(a) AUTHORIZATION- The President is authorized, subject to subsection (b), to the United States Armed Forces pursuant to United Nations Security Council Resolution 678 (1990) in order to achieve implementation of Security Council Resolutions 660, 661, 662, 664, 665, 666, 667, 669, 670, 674, and 677.

(b) REQUIREMENTS FOR DETERMINATION THAT USE OF MILITARY FORCE IS NECESSARY- Be fore exercising the authority granted in subsection (a), the President shall make available to the Speaker and the House of Representatives and the President pro tempore of the Senate his determination that—

(1) The United States has used all appropriate diplomatic and other peaceful means to obtain compliance by Iraq with the United Nations Security Council resolutions cited in subsection (a); and

(2) Those efforts have not been and would not be successful in obtaining such compliance.

The resolution continued on to refer to the War Powers Resolution as the specific legal reference for this "statutory authorization."

This resolution was passed, predominantly along a party-line vote. The vote was 52 "yes" to 47 "no". The "no" vote was made up of 45 Democrats and 2 Republicans. Senator Kerry was among this group. In the "yes" vote Republicans were joined by 10 Democrats. Oddly, Senator Kerry, speaking on the floor of the Senate, claimed of his "no" vote:

"It is a vote about war because whether or not the president exercises his power, we will have no further say after this vote."

He complained that Congress would have "no further say." Ironically, he was in favor of the first resolution that would have stripped Congress of any further say by favoring a "declaration" of war instead of the "statutory authorization" of the second, passed, resolution in which Congress would retain the powers it created for itself in the War Powers Resolution.

Senator Kerry's inconsistent logic regarding his votes for the 1991 Gulf War continued into the next decade, when it came time to vote for the use of military force in Iraq, for a seemingly weaker cause. In 1991, the invasion of Iraq had been prompted by the overt act of Iraq's invasion and subsequent occupation of Kuwait. In 2002, the main reasoning for the use of military force was in reaction to Iraq's potential to do harm, not an overt hostile act. Yet, Senator Kerry voted for the "statutory authorization" to employ military force against Iraq in 2002 after earlier voting against "statutory authorization" in 1991.

Two months after voting in favor of granting the president permission to use military force in Iraq, while appearing on NBC's Meet the Press, Senator Kerry expressed his intent to form an "exploratory committee" in anticipation of becoming a candidate for president for the 2004 election. Senator Kerry's position on the war in Iraq evolved over the nearly two years between his December 2002 announcement on Meet the Press and the November 2004 election. As late as May of 2003, Senator Kerry asserted that the vote to authorize military force in Iraq was the "right decision." Coincidentally, second quarter fund raising reports for the announced Democratic Party candidates for president showed Governor Dean as the early leader. Dean's strong anti-war position seems to have caused an "evolution" among the other candidates, including Senator Kerry. While the other candidates did not immediately become anti-war, at least they began to differentiate themselves with President Bush.

By January of 2004, Senator Kerry began to run as a full-fledged anti-war candidate in the lead up to the Iowa Caucuses on the 19th of January. Senator Kerry said: "I don't believe the president took us to war as he should have." The statement enabled Kerry to continue to hold that his vote to authorize the use of military force was still the right one while criticizing the president's methods. The wording of the original resolution which called for the president to report to Congress on matters related to "further diplomatic or other peaceful means" allowed anyone to second guess the timing and extent of military action. It was very easy for even supporters of the resolution to distance themselves from President Bush's decision to use military force by simply saying we should have spent just a little more time to "give peace a chance."

Senator Kerry's "nuanced" position was apparently rewarded, and encouraged, by the results of the Iowa Caucuses - he won. Governor Dean's considerable campaign effort in Iowa, along with his success raising money, had failed. The Iowa results were perhaps reflective, too, of the national mood toward the war. Pew Research Center polls taken in March 2004, showed that 55 percent of the people believed the decision to use military force was the "right decision" while only 39 percent felt that it was wrong. In the same poll, 61 percent believed the war was going well, compared to 37 percent that felt it was not. These results, more than the infamous "Dean Scream" would seem to indicate why Governor Dean failed to resonate with the Iowa Democrats attending the caucuses.

The polls leading up the November election reflected a closing of the gap between those who felt the decision to use force was correct and those that did not. For the remainder of the campaign the percentage of those feeling the decision was correct remained above 50 percent while the percentage of those who felt the war was going well hovered near 50 percent. By the time of the political conventions it is not clear whether the candidate was leading public opinion or whether public opinion was leading the candidate. A week after receiving the nomination at the late July convention in Boston, Senator Kerry reaffirmed his original vote by saying: "Yes, I would have voted for the authority. I believe it was the right authority for a president to have." However he added: "Although I would have done this very differently from the way President Bush has."

Nuance and equivocation failed to get Senator Kerry elected president in 2004; however, it did point the way to the Democratic Party for the ensuing four years leading to the midterm election of 2006 and the presidential campaign and election of 2008. Soon after the 2004 election in which President Bush was reelected a collective amnesia came over many in Congress that had voted for the "statutory authorization" of military force. Virtually all provisions in the authorization bill that were used to justify the military force in Iraq were forgotten, that is, with the exception of the provisions having to do with weapons of mass destruction (WMD). The failure to find mass stockpiles of chemical and biological weapons, coupled with a failure to prove that an active nuclear weapons development program existed immediately prior to the 2003 invasion, provided a new wedge issue to exploit for political purposes. Within the year following the 2004 election, candidates were already jockeying for position and advantage.

Among the first candidates to show interest in running for the office of president in 2008 was John Edwards, John Kerry's vice presidential running mate. As John Edwards had not run for reelection to the U.S. Senate in 2004, he was now free to pursue his own causes and lay the foundation for a presidential campaign.

As a senator during the 107th Congress, Senator Edwards had been one of the 77 senators to vote in favor of providing statutory authorization to use military force in Iraq. Although Edwards, the vice presidential candidate, followed John Kerry's lead by stating that his vote was the "right decision", by November 2005, he had changed his strategy. In an op-ed piece published November 13th, 2005, Edwards stated in part:

> "I was wrong.
>
> Almost three years ago we went into Iraq to remove what we were told – and what many of us believed and argued – was a threat to America. But, in fact, we now know that Iraq did not have weapons of mass destruction when our forces invaded Iraq in 2003. The intelligence was deeply flawed and, in some cases, manipulated to fit a political agenda.
>
> It was a mistake to vote for the war in 2002. I take responsibility for that mistake. It has been hard to say these words because those who didn't make a mistake – the men and women of our armed forces and their families – have performed heroically and paid a dear price.
>
> The world desperately needs moral leadership from America, and the foundation for moral leadership is telling the truth.
>
> While we can't change the past, we need to accept responsibility, because a key part of restoring America's moral leadership is acknowledging when we've made mistakes or been proven wrong – and showing that we have the creativity and guts to make it right.
>
> The argument for going to war with Iraq was based on the intelligence that we now know was inaccurate. The information the American people were hearing from the president – and that I was being given by our intelligence community – wasn't the whole story. Had I known this at the time, I never would have voted for this war.

George Bush won't accept responsibility for his mistakes. Along with Dick Cheney and Donald Rumsfeld, he has made horrible mistakes at almost every step: failed diplomacy; not going in with enough troops; not giving our forces the equipment they need; not having a plan for peace.

Because of these failures, Iraq is a mess and has become a far greater threat than it ever was. It is now a haven for terrorists, and our presence there is draining the goodwill our country once enjoyed, diminishing our global standing. It has made fighting the global war against terrorist organizations more difficult, not less."

John Edwards' article became the template for members of Congress to take political advantage leading into the 2006 and 2008 elections. Many of his assertions were to be employed repeatedly over the next three years and two political campaigns. The major points that found their way into the media and congressional as well as presidential politics were:

- No weapons of mass destruction
- Flawed intelligence
- Intelligence manipulated for political purposes
- The president lied
- Loss of American moral leadership
- Failure to admit mistakes
- Had I known then what I know now...
- George Bush, Dick Cheney, and Donald Rumsfeld made mistakes that they will not admit to
- Failed diplomacy
- Not enough troops
- Inadequate equipment
- No plan for peace
- Iraq is a mess
- Loss of global standing
- War on terror more difficult as a result of Iraq

Besides using a new line to curry favor with voters by saying that "he was wrong," John Edwards also borrowed a ploy he learned from John Kerry – he commended the bravery and resilience of the military and their families. In attempting to immunize themselves from criticism that they were not "supporting the troops," Edwards made criticisms of the president and the war strategy "acceptable" provided the criticisms were prefaced by trite words of support for the troops. Members of Congress who had learned to hate the military during the Viet Nam War now learned to give the troops a "pat on the head" with one hand while bashing the Commander-in-Chief with the other hand.

By the time that the 2008 presidential campaign took shape the criticism of the war among the various candidates reached "feeding frenzy" dimensions. The early front-runner for the Democratic Party nomination, Senator Hillary Clinton, was hounded by the press and anti-war groups like Code Pink to make statements similar to those made by John Edwards, especially to admit she was "wrong" in voting to authorize the use of military force in Iraq. By 2007, Senator Clinton's position had evolved to the point where she was making the "if I knew then what I know now…" comment with regard to her affirmative vote.

Most candidates, Republican and Democrat alike, condemned the actions of President Bush. Claims were made that President Bush had "cooked" the intelligence somehow in order to hoodwink Congress into approving the use of force. President Bush was accused of promoting a war for political purposes. All candidates, regardless of prior military experience of their own, became self-proclaimed experts on military strategy and tactics. Each candidate, with the benefit of 20/20 hindsight, had a plan for how the war should have been prosecuted and how it should be going forward in the post-Saddam Iraq.

Some candidates had the luxury of saying "I told you so." One candidate, who ultimately was elected president, had the double luxury of saying "I told you so" and not having to participate in the 2002 vote. U.S. Representative Ron Paul, a Texas Republican, had strongly opposed the war's authorization. In a speech delivered on the floor of the House on October 8th 2002, Congressman Paul said the following:

"... This is not a resolution to declare war. We know that. This is a resolution that does something much different. This resolution transfers the responsibility, the authority, and the power of the Congress to the President so he can declare war when and if he wants to. He has not even indicated that he wants to go to war or has to go to war; but he will make the full decision, not the Congress, not the people through the Congress of this country in that manner."

Illinois state senator, Barrack Obama, made his own October 2002 speech of opposition at the Federal Plaza in Chicago. In explaining his opposition he said:

"I don't oppose all wars. What I am opposed to is a dumb war. What I am opposed to is a rash war. What I am opposed to is the cynical attempt by Richard Perle and Paul Wolfowitz and other armchair, weekend warriors in this administration to shove their own ideological agendas down our throats, irrespective of the costs in lives lost and in hardships borne.

What I am opposed to is the attempt by political hacks like Karl Rove to distract us from a rise in the uninsured, a rise in the poverty rate, a drop in the median income, to distract us from corporate scandals and a stock market that has just gone through the worst month since the Great Depression.

That's what I'm opposed to. A dumb war. A rash war. A war based not on reason but on passion, not on principle but on politics."

Senator John McCain, the ultimate Republican presidential candidate in 2008, criticized the war from the opposite direction. He was among those in Congress who did not apologize for his 2002 vote or admit he had been wrong; however, this did not stop him from criticizing the prosecution of the war. He felt the President had not used enough force. He became a strong proponent of increasing troop levels in Iraq in the period preceding the 2008 election. In remarks liberally taken out of context by the press and his Democratic Party opponents, McCain compared a U.S. commitment to Iraq as being similar to the long term commitment to South Korea, Japan and Germany. He expressed a willingness to accept having troops in Iraq for "100 years", if necessary, to accomplish the objectives being pursued by the United States in Iraq.

It is not my intent to recount the 2008 election as a national referendum on the war in Iraq. It is my point to show how the war became entangled in partisan politics that undermined the support of the war by the people and undermined the progress of the military actions being taken in Iraq. The War Powers Resolution under which "statutory authorization" for the war was granted by Congress, aided and abetted a systematic process by which the Congress abdicated its Constitutional responsibilities, while at the same time, providing members of Congress the ability to second-guess and criticize the decisions made by President Bush. The War Powers Resolution enabled each member of Congress and each candidate for president to become, in Senator Obama's words, an "armchair warrior" without consequence.

The campaign of 2008 was largely poll-driven as opposed to principles-driven. Senator McCain intentionally distanced himself from President Bush in an attempt to appeal to independent voters and moderates within his own party. Senator Obama, aided by his 2002 position, tacked further to the left than the opponents in his own party could. His presidential primary opponents, like Mrs. Clinton, were burdened by their vote in 2002. Apologies and denials were incapable of winning over the anti-war left base of the Democratic Party.

Once elected, President Obama was able to follow the stream of reasoning employed during the campaign. Without the clear statement that would have been provided by a formal declaration of war by Congress, the statutory authorization provided under the War Powers Resolution provided the new president with enough wiggle room to redefine the war as something other than a war. As President Truman's "police action" in Korea before, euphemisms, such as "foreign contingency operations" replaced stronger, more "offensive" terms for the many armed unpleasantries the United States was involved with around the world. The term "War on Terror" was dropped from the vernacular completely. Organized, centrally controlled, acts of terror perpetrated by Arab Muslims against civilians were reduced to "law enforcements matters" by the anonymous stroke of a pen. The War Powers Resolution has provided the ultimate "trap door." The trap door is no longer reserved exclusively for Congress. The trap door is now open to the president as well.

Taking the Eye off the Ball

The War Powers Resolution of 1973 was only the first step in formalizing our "new" approach to fighting wars. The confluence of events and movements of the mid-70s also marked a major shift in how the United States regards its military. Societal changes that collided in the early 1970s led to a shift away from "mission orientation" to "political orientation" of the military. The impact of the changes begun in the early 70s has a profound influence on our present day military. Our ability to fight and win wars was and remains severely undermined.

Aside from the anti-war movement, the abandonment of Viet Nam in 1975, and the ensuing demoralization of the American military, the future course of the American military was also shaped by other seemingly unrelated events.

- The Watergate scandal severely weakened the president's ability to act as a coequal branch of government.
- The 1972 proposal of an Equal Rights Amendment to the Constitution; the Supreme Court's landmark decision on abortion in 1973; and a radical feminist movement, put the rights and roles of women in society at the forefront of national debate.
- The end of the draft and the beginning of the "all volunteer" military began a process of "distancing" between the military and the American people.
- The civil rights legislation of the 1960s entered into an enforcement phase in the early 70s with racial integration and affirmative action programs.

Congress, emboldened by the demise of the Nixon presidency, reacted to these "seemingly unrelated" matters by asserting its Constitutional power over the military by transforming the military into a veritable "laboratory for social change." Frustrated by the slow progress of racial integration and affirmative action and by the failure to gain the ratification of the Equal Rights Amendment by the states, Congress set out to impose its will on the military. The election of a liberal, one-term governor, Jimmy Carter, as the first post Viet Nam/post Watergate president, further enabled the transformation of the military from a mission oriented force to the politically oriented force of today.

Apparently wishing to set a national example for the states, the Congress imposed major cultural changes on an organization whose customs, traditions and standards were formed even before the birth of the nation. Changes were made without regard to any of these customs, traditions or standards. Most importantly, no consideration was given to the impact the imposition of these cultural changes would have on the readiness of the military to fight and win wars – zip, zero, nada.

Women in the Military

As a First Class (senior class) Midshipman at the Naval Academy, I was present "at the table" during the discussions of how the Naval Academy would integrate women for the first time in its history. Our discussions were wide-ranging; however, we were always herded back onto the practical and away from the philosophical, the philosophical aspects of integrating women were not open for discussion. For example, we discussed in detail which dormitory rooms could and could not accommodate women. Women would not be subjected to living in rooms on courtyards in order to protect them from window peeping male midshipmen. We also discussed separate standards for testing physical strength and endurance as well as necessary modifications from everything from the obstacle course to the barbershop.

When we raised questions about the potential for male-female relationships that might prove contrary to "good order and discipline;" the "mission of the Academy;" or even the "mission of the Navy", we were told that the decision was made at a "higher level." It was now our duty to carry out the orders of the civilian leadership of the government. During those days leading up to the admission of women to the service academies frequently were uttered the words of English poet laureate, Alfred Tennyson, in his classic poem, *Charge of the Light Brigade*: "Theirs not to make reply, Theirs not to reason why, Theirs but to do or die."

The admission of women into the service academies began during the summer of 1976. While not the first women to serve in the military, the young women who entered the military services starting in the mid-70s, were the first to serve, where military careers and career advancement among women was made a higher priority than mission readiness. Even though the Equal Rights Amendment was never "ratified by Legislatures of three-fourths of the several States," it became the law of the land in the military. A group, originally formed in 1951, The Defense Department Advisory Committee on Women in the Services (DACOWITS), became a militant force within the Defense Department, promoting military careerism for women in heretofore male only roles. DACOWITS, predominantly made up of civilians and academics, goaded Congress and the Defense Department into subordinating mission readiness to the career aspirations of women in the services. Although DACOWITS' influence on the political process has somewhat diminished since its charter and Federal funding were permitted to lapse in 2002, it continues to be an advocate for greater career opportunities for women serving in the military. A review of their current areas of concern shows there is little concern for military combat readiness and near total concern for career viability of women.

The following is taken from the DACOWITS official website and their self-described topics of interest:

In order to provide tomorrow's generation of female Service members with a roadmap to success, and to augment the information available to military planners, DACOWITS seeks to gather lessons learned from current female leaders regarding the strategies that have helped them to reach their goals in the military.

- What are the career barriers that women Service members encounter, or have encountered, and how have they changed over time?
- Which strategies have been most successful at helping women overcome career barriers and promoting their success and how have these success strategies changed over time?
- How do success strategies differ for women at different points in their careers?
- To what extent do the success strategies that helped today's senior officers and enlisted women (e.g., 05, E7 and above?) apply to today's junior female Service members? (e.g., 01-03 and E1-E4?)
- What strategies are employed in the military specifically to develop female leaders, and how do they work?

This example is merely a brief accounting of the central policy priorities surrounding the issue of women in the military. In no way do I wish to imply that women in the military are homogeneously incompetent. What I do wish to say is that a large number of women are in the military for the wrong reasons and that military readiness would be better served by policy priorities that are focused on combat readiness not on career viability.

Congress has attempted the impossible – the legislative repeal of the laws of nature. Congress and their occasional accomplices in the Executive branch of government have believed that human behavior within the military can be completely regulated by government. The civilian leadership, now almost completely void of firsthand military experience, has not a clue of the differences between male-only military units opposed to male-female military units. They seem not to realize that human relations between men and women that we wish to foster in the basic societal unit, the family, cannot be erased by legislative fiat in military units. In attempting to legislate male-female relations in the military the civilian leadership brings about the unintended consequence of degraded mission readiness. Military units are best prepared for combat when comprised of men and men only. Military units are by nature asexual. The imposition of women (or openly gay men) onto the military culture disrupts this nature.

The best way to characterize a military unit of men for those who have not served in one is to call it a "brotherhood." A bond forms among men in this brotherhood. When properly channeled through the judicious application of leadership, this bond creates a collective force that is capable of performing otherwise impossible acts of selfless courage, physical strength, and individual endurance. With a legislative fiat, orders of superiors, and sensitivity training to the contrary, this bond is weakened, if not unglued, when women are inserted into this brotherhood.

Heretofore, Congress has resisted the persistent urgings of organizations, like DACOWITS, to integrate women into virtually all aspects of military life. Bowing to the recommendations of military professionals, Congress has not yet authorized measures such as the modification of submarine designs in order to accommodate mixed gender crews. Nevertheless, women are now integrated into the majority of military units, not as a way of improving readiness but rather to ensure that women remain competitive with their male counterparts for promotion opportunities.

Affirmative Action

A close "relative" to the integration of women into the military is Affirmative Action. While the integration of women is an affirmative action program in and of itself, affirmative action is normally considered as a separate and distinct, male only, issue within the military. Affirmative action in the military is almost exclusively a creature of the officer corps. In general, the enlisted corps within the various services is comprised of a percentage of racial and ethnic minority personnel that is equal to or exceeds the percentage in the general population. Furthermore, promotion within the enlisted ranks is generally based on the demonstration of job performance by measurable means. There is near universal perception that promotion within the enlisted ranks is based almost entirely on merit. As a consequence, minority personnel can earn promotion to positions of greater pay and responsibility with the full acceptance of their non-minority subordinates and peers.

Unlike the enlisted corps, the officer corps is almost entirely comprised of college educated men. Using a college degree as an initial "term of employment" a large percentage of the minority population is already excluded. The manpower pool is dramatically reduced. Since there is a widespread, (I believe deeply flawed) belief that the officer corps should more closely reflect the enlisted corps which it leads, there is a very active affirmative action program to recruit, educate, train, and promote minority officers.

Unlike their counterparts in the enlisted ranks, officers are evaluated far more subjectively. Qualities and qualifications of officers are frequently far more difficult to measure using quantitative methods such as written exams and practical demonstrations of skills. As a consequence of this subjectivity, the perception among many within both the officer and enlisted corps that affirmative action brings about the promotion of inferior officers, or at least the promotion of officers, prematurely.

Affirmative action has a sinister effect on the entire military, especially in officer communities that rely almost totally on subjective evaluation of performance. Affirmative action policies have an insidious effect on multiple fronts.

Affirmative action undermines the self-esteem of each minority officer. All minority officers, regardless of their professional abilities and qualifications, wonder whether or not their accomplishments, their career progress, their rank promotions, are due to their own merit or affirmative action. The problem does not get better over time, if anything it gets worse. As officers ascend to positions of greater authority, greater responsibility and higher rank, the pressure placed on selection boards by Congress and senior Defense Department officials to promote minority officers becomes intense. Consequently, minority officers are promoted ahead of their peers for no other apparent reason than affirmative action. As a result, the promoted minority officer may be advanced to a position he is not qualified or otherwise prepared for by his experience. Failure is often the result, failure that serves neither readiness nor the officer in question. It is the "Peter Principle" run amuck.

Minority officers lose respect from subordinates, peers and superiors who may be dubious about that officer's professional qualifications, thereby undermining that officer's authority. Confidence is a major component of leadership, especially in the military where the work is often demanding if not dangerous. In order for an officer to be effective during demanding times, he not only needs self-confidence but he also needs the confidence of his subordinates, his peers, and his superiors. The lack of confidence at one or more of these four levels can make for potential disaster.

Affirmative action can bring about the loss of one or more of these elements of confidence either by perception or by reality. If at any level, an officer is suspected of achieving his position of authority by means other than merit, his authority and credibility are undermined. On the other hand, if, by way of affirmative action, an unqualified officer is promoted to a position of authority prematurely, when subjected to the bright lights of demanding military action, confidence will be lost. Loss of confidence during military operations is potentially coincidental to mission failure. Mission failure can result in more than falling short of goals. Mission failure can result in costly damage to equipment, or worse, injury or death of personnel.

Finally, affirmative action policies undermine readiness by recruiting, educating, training and promoting substandard officers. I have been reminded of this aspect of affirmative action recently by statements made by the Chief of Naval Operations, Admiral Gary Roughead and the Superintendent of the Naval Academy, Vice Admiral Jeffrey L. Fowler related to the "highest priority" for the Naval Academy – "DIVERSITY." Admiral Roughead stated that "diversity is the number one priority" and Vice Admiral Fowler included that "Everyone understands that "diversity" here means nonwhite skins." Welcome Naval Academy Class of 2013! You are now marked for life as an affirmative action accession.

Diversity

The current Naval Academy diversity drive presents an excellent case-study into the wisdom (or folly) of pursuing racial/ethnic quotas, especially in a mission oriented, war fighting organization. The Naval Academy example is useful in analyzing the other services as well since the other services, with the exception of the Army, have roughly the same percentage of white officers serving on active duty. If one is to believe the Chief of Naval Operations and the Superintendent of the Naval Academy, it is the white officers that present the problem that needs to be solved.

Recent articles from both official Academy reports, as well as opinion/editorial pieces, written on the subject of diversity at the Naval Academy have not always been specific with the underlying demographic statistics. The following demographic statistics are taken from the most current U.S. Census and Department of the Navy reports. According to U.S. Census data estimates for 2008, there were a total of 304,059,724 people living in the United States. Of those, approximately 66 percent are White; 15 percent are Hispanic/Latino; 13 percent are Black; 1 percent is American Indian/Native Alaskan; and the remaining 5 percent are mostly Asian and Pacific Islanders.

According to data taken from the Defense Manpower Data Center Report 3035EO for September 2008, the following percentages apply to the Navy alone. The Navy's population at the time of the report was 325,031. Of that total end strength 275,296, (85%) are enlisted and 49,735 (15%) are officers. The Defense Department does not consider Hispanics and Latinos as a separate and distinct racial group but rather as an ethnic group. Hispanics are mainly lumped into the totals under the White racial category. Besides the "White" racial category, the Defense Department divides its personnel into six other distinct racial groupings – Black, American Indian/Alaskan Native, Asian, Pacific Islander, Multiple and Unknown racial backgrounds.

The issue that is apparently causing the CNO and the Superintendent to lose sleep at night is caused by the fact that the percentage of enlisted sailors identified as "Black" is 20.7 percent of the total while Black officers comprise only 7.8 percent of the total officer corps in the Navy. It should be noted that the percentage of Black enlisted sailors exceeds the percentage in the general population by roughly 8 percentage points. There appears to be somewhat less concern for the 16 percent of sailors who are considered ethnic Hispanics. There is only a 1 percentage point difference between the Navy Hispanic population and the 15 percent in the general population. This grouping seems to be largely incorporated into the White racial cohort.

While the combined population of the "other" racial groups is the largest minority group in the Navy, roughly 18 percent, there appears to be little concern for whether or not these racial groups are properly represented in the officer corps. It becomes clear that the Superintendent's statement: "Everyone understands that "diversity" here means nonwhite skins" means affirmative action is for primarily Black candidates. It has become more important to size the officer corps to fit a disproportionately large Black component in the volunteer Navy than to better balance the force to fall more in line with the general population.

While U.S. Census data indicates 34 percent of the population is a racial or ethnic minority, the Naval Academy's official announcement, entitled **Admissions Diversity**, claims that this percentage is 40 percent. In the announcement for the incoming Class of 2013 the Naval Academy trumpets that 35 percent of the class will be made up of ethnic and racial minorities. Of this group 14 percent will be Hispanic and 10 percent will be African American. The official Naval Academy announcement went on to claim that "every candidate competes equally in a single highly-selective and competitive admissions process... Everyone admitted to the Academy is fully qualified morally, mentally, and physically." The announcement went on to say that "the Naval Academy chose Hispanics whose average SAT score is in the top 5% of all college-bound Hispanics and African Americans whose SAT score is in the top 6% of all college-bound African Americans." These official statements essentially admit a two-tier, double standard, admissions policy by comparing these two minority groups against themselves rather than the overall pool of applicants to the Academy.

Admissions officials at the Academy proudly report that they have made new inroads in underrepresented areas and school districts, such as New York City, the nation's largest public school district. Unfortunately, what the admissions people fail to mention is that the New York school district has among the worst graduation rates in the country, 50.5 percent, and that New York ranks 45th out of 51 in combined SAT scores nationally. The admissions officials fail to add that African Americans and Hispanics typically performing 20 percent below college-bound White students. In other words, the "cherry picking" of candidates claim is of dubious value.

The diversity initiative at the Naval Academy was thrust into the limelight by way of a guest column published in the June 14th 2009 Annapolis Capital, the Maryland capital's main newspaper. The article, written by Professor Bruce Fleming, a 22 year tenured English professor at the Academy, claimed that:

> Midshipmen are admitted by two tracks. White applicants out of high school who are not also athletic recruits typically need grades of A and B and minimum SAT scores of 600 on each part for the (Admissions) Board to vote them "qualified." Athletics and leadership also count.

> A vote of "qualified" for a white applicant doesn't mean s/he's coming, only that he or she can compete to win the "slate" of up to 10 nominations that (most typically) a Congress(wo)man draws up. That means that nine "qualified" white applicants are rejected. SAT scores below 600 or C grades almost always produce a vote of "not qualified" for white applicants.

> Not so for an applicant who self-identifies as one of the minorities who are our "number one priority." For them, another set of rules apply. Their cases are briefed separately to the board, and SAT scores to the mid-500s with quite a few Cs in classes (and no visible athletics or leadership) typically produce a vote of "qualified" for them, with direct admission to Annapolis. They're in, and are given a pro forma nomination to make it legit.

> Minority applicants with scores and grades down to the 300s with Cs and Ds (and no particular leadership or athletics) also come, though after a remedial year at our taxpayer-supported remedial school, the Naval Academy Preparatory School (NAPS).

By using NAPS as a feeder, we've virtually eliminated all competition for "diverse" candidates; in theory they have to get a C average at NAPS to come to USNA, but this is regularly re-negotiated.

All this is probably unconstitutional. That's what the Supreme Court said about the University of Michigan's two-track admissions in 2003.

Once at Annapolis, "diverse" midshipmen are over-represented in our pre-college classes, in lower track course, in mandatory tutoring programs and less challenging majors. Many struggle to master basic concepts. (I teach some of these courses).

Of course, some minority students are stellar, but they're the exception. Despite being dragged toward the finish line, minorities graduate at about 10 percent lower rate than the whole class, which, of course, includes them (so the real split is greater).

Professor Fleming expanded on his Annapolis Capital comments when he was interviewed by Daniel de Vise for the July 3rd 2009 Washington Post. He stated that: "First of all, we're dumbing down the Naval Academy. Second of all, we are dumbing down the officer corps."

In response to Professor Fleming's assertions, Dr. William Miller, Academic Dean and Provost of the Naval Academy commented to Mr. de Vise that: "This class we inducted yesterday may be the most talented overall that we have ever brought into the Naval Academy. We have increased the standards, rather than dumbing them down."

No mention is made in the Washington Post article that Dean Miller is a retired Navy Rear Admiral and 1962 graduate of the Naval Academy himself. Dean Miller's comments are not original. Every incoming class at the Naval Academy is told they are the "most talented," "best qualified," class in Academy history. Unfortunately, due to Dean Miller's long association with the Naval Academy first as a midshipman and during his naval career as an electrical engineering instructor and Executive Assistant to the Superintendent, he is far less likely to be an impartial observer of the Academy's change in priorities than is Professor Fleming. Dean Miller is likely to be every bit as much of a "yes man" on the issue of diversity as are Admirals Roughead and Fowler. Another point regarding the Academic Dean is that he is a product of the Navy rather than Academia. Unlike his counterparts in other colleges and universities, he is naturally inclined toward loyalty to the service rather than to the concept of academic freedom. He is far more likely to "go along to get along" than he is to being constructively critical of practices and policies detrimental to scholarship.

Seeking to confirm or deny Professor Fleming's claims, especially regarding the Naval Academy Prep School, I attempted to contact the military commanding officer of the Prep School as well as its civilian academic dean. As a NAPS alumnus myself and former instructor there, I, perhaps naively, assumed that this would be an easy matter. Within days of requesting comments regarding Professor Fleming's claims as well as rumors I had heard from various sources, I received a response from the Naval Academy's Public Affairs Office.

Let it suffice to say, after several months of e-mail exchanges with various people affiliated with public affairs, I am inclined to believe everything Professor Fleming had to say about diversity at the Naval Academy and the Prep School. Had the Naval Academy been willing to address my concerns forthrightly and in a timely manner, I may have come away with a different assessment. Instead I have come away with a visceral feeling that they are attempting to hide something. I am left to make some conclusions based on what I think rather than what I know for sure. I regret that.

Perhaps the best way to illustrate the folly of the drift away from a "mission oriented" Naval Academy toward a "diversity oriented" Naval Academy is with a sports analogy. Sports, historically, have been highly emphasized at the various service academies. It is felt that sports provide the best, non-lethal, way to prepare men for combat. Sports replicate many aspects of armed conflict. Sports are reciprocal in nature, just like Clausewitz informs us, is true of armed conflict. Sports have two sides, offense and defense, each side struggling against the other for advantage. Sports are also about winning.

"Winning isn't everything, it's the only thing." A statement made famous by a former West Point assistant football coach by the name of Vince Lombardi, expresses for many, the essence of sports in America. Shortly after taking over as West Point's first post World War I Superintendent, General Douglas MacArthur had the following words carved in the stone portals above the West Point gymnasium:

"Upon the fields of friendly strife
Are sown the seeds
That, upon other fields, on other days
Will bear the fruits of victory"

General MacArthur, having recently returned from the battlefields of Europe, understood the value of sports and physical training in preparing men for victory in battle. In a closely related statement of philosophy, MacArthur's personal motto would become:

"In war, there is no substitute for victory."

So how does this sports analogy relate to diversity at the Naval Academy and more broadly to affirmative action in the military?

In sports, where winning is the "only thing," there is a direct parallel with the philosophy in war, where "victory" is the only thing. Whereas "winning" is the single focus of professional sports teams, so too, should it be that "victory" in war be the single focus of a professional military. Since we already know that the Naval Academy has made diversity its "number one priority," it might be interesting to see how a professional sports team with "winning" as its number one priority uses diversity to achieve its goal.

For the purpose of this purely unscientific survey, I chose my hometown teams the New England Patriots, the Boston Red Sox, the Boston Celtics, and the Boston Bruins. As my luck would have it, all four teams have had considerable success at winning in the recent past.

I turn first to the New England Patriots because their Head Coach, Bill Belichick, and I have a special affinity. Bill's dad was an assistant football coach at the Naval Academy and Bill grew up in Annapolis. He spent his formative years in football at the Academy about the same time I was a midshipman. Surely, if diversity were important to winning, Coach Belichick would employ it on the Patriots.

In taking a "snap-shot" of the New England roster, I found that of the 86 players (think enlisted men) currently listed on the main roster and practice squad, 32 players (37.2%) are White. The remaining 54 players (62.8%) are Black. Of the top management and coaching staff (think officers) of 20 men, 17 are White (85%) and 3 are Black (15%). None of the players, none of the coaches and none of the top managers are women.

I then looked at the 25-man roster of the Red Sox. There are 19 White players; 1 American Indian (Jacoby Ellsbury, first American Indian of Navajo descent to reach the major leagues); 2 Japanese; and, 3 from the Dominican Republic, no African Americans, and no women. Of the Manager and his 6 primary assistants, there is 1 African American and 6 Whites. Although I could not verify it photographically, it appears that the ownership and management staff is almost entirely White.

The Boston Celtics presently has a roster of 17 players. There is 1 White (6%) among 16 Black players (94%). The coaching staff, led by Doc Rivers, who is Black, is comprised of 3 Black assistants, 3 Whites and 1 Asian.

The Boston Bruins are completely White; however, I found it interesting that of the 21 players on the roster, only 4 (19%) players are American. The majority of the team is made up of 14 (66%) from Canada and 3 (14%) from Europe. The coaching staff and the top management staff are made up of White men, many from Canada.

With the exception of the Red Sox, with their two Japanese, one American Indian, and three Latin Americans, none of the four New England professional teams have Asians, Pacific Islanders, or American Indian/Alaskans on their player rosters. With the exception of some administrative staff personnel, there are virtually no women in management positions in these, <u>all</u> <u>male</u>, teams.

There are several obvious observations that can be derived from this "snapshot" of four major professional teams. First, there is little or no regard for diversity, trying to "reflect America," or even the region in which they play. Very few of the players on the New England teams are from New England. Second, there is total commitment to winning. Judging from the sale of season tickets and sold-out contests, it would appear that the fans have no objection to this winning strategy. Winning at war should have the same commitment from our President, from our Congress, and from the "season ticket holders" of the military, the taxpaying citizens of the United States. Building a winning military should follow the same principles that professional sports follow – put the best possible "players" on the field.

Professional sports can also provide a window into more than just winning. Sports can tell us about the necessity for leaders to come from the same race or ethnic background of the majority of their players. Bill Belichick, one of the most successful coaches of our time, is neither black nor is he a former NFL player. He is a professional leader.

Leadership is comprised of a combination of qualities. Some of those qualities are natural and many qualities can be gained through education and training of willing students. The best leaders come to the service academies out of a desire to serve selflessly, not out of a desire for a free college education. The best leaders knew about West Point, Annapolis, Colorado Springs, and New London before they entered middle school. They did not learn about these places for the first time from a recruiter visiting their school during their junior year in high school.

Sports can also tell us a lot about self-selecting, volunteer, organizations like pro teams and like the military service. For a complex series of reasons people choose to play certain sports and people choose to serve in the military. While there may be some athletes that are "forced" into participation by their parents, most athletes who end up on professional teams get there through self-determination and dedication to excellence in their sports. The same thing can be said about service men and women. Those young men and women who lack dedication and self-determination to become effective warriors quickly learn that they are poorly suited for military service.

What is it that makes Black athletes gravitate toward football and basketball but not baseball and hockey? What is it that makes Canadians more interested in hockey than Americans? Why do only a few New Englanders play professional baseball? Why do a higher percentage of Texans (6.822 per 10,000 people) join the military than from Massachusetts (3.058 per 10,000 people)? Why is that only a hand full of Ivy League college graduates volunteer to serve in the military each year?

The Chief of Naval Operations and the Superintendent of the Naval Academy are well intended in their wishes to have a Brigade of Midshipmen that "looks more like America, and better represents the nation it serves." The only problem is they have misidentified the source of the problem. They are attempting to correct the wrong problem with the wrong solutions. Before they can successfully recruit a more representative class they first must recruit a more representative Navy. The Navy, and by extension all the services, does not currently look like, or act like, America, and that is the problem.

The All-Volunteer Force is a Failure

Congressman Charles Rangel of the 15th District of New York is a rarity in the Congress, he is a combat veteran. He was decorated for service in the Korean War. As Chairman of the House Ways and Means Committee, he is among the most powerful members of Congress. He speaks with strength on matters related to the military. In January of 2003, Congressman Rangel began promoting a plan to reinstitute the military draft. In 2004, his bill was defeated by a vote of 402 to 2. Representative Rangel, claiming that the vote was brought about by the Republican leadership "playing games," voted against his own bill. Nevertheless, Rangel makes some good points about the all-volunteer force.

In his original bill, submitted after the 2002 Authorization for use of Military Force Against Iraq Resolution but before the 2003 invasion of Iraq, Rangel made several points. He stated that he introduced the bill "in hopes that those people who make the decisions to go to war to attack Iraq, would be better influenced against it if they had kids that would be placed in harm's way, or if they felt closer to the shared sacrifice that we oftentimes talk about."

Rangel's main case, reflecting his own bias and predominantly African American constituency, was that a disproportionate number of military personnel came "from the lower economic levels of our society" and furthermore, more than 30 percent of the forces were made up of racial and ethnic minorities. Rangel was almost totally dismissed for trying to recycle old, Viet Nam era, arguments. The Defense Secretary, Donald Rumsfeld, while not addressing Congressman Rangel's claims about economic and racial disparities in the volunteer military force, reassured us that there was no need for a draft because the military was able to attract a sufficient number of recruits without one. He also asserted at the same time that "disadvantages of using compulsion to bring into the armed forces the men and women needed are notable." Both men were right.

While Congressman Rangel's claims about the economic background of the armed forces have been widely discredited by organizations like the Heritage Foundation, he is correct in implying that few in the current force come from affluent backgrounds. He is also correct in stating that there is an imbalance in minority representation in the military. Of the racial and ethnic minority groups tracked by the Defense Department, Black enlisted men and women as well as Native Americans make up a greater percentage in the military than they do in society. In the four branches of the military and the Coast Guard, Black enlisted personnel make up 18.3 percent of the force, 5.5 percent above the percentage within the overall population. For Native Americans the percentage is 0.9 percent greater than within the overall population.

It can be, and has been, argued that all military members since the end of the draft in 1973 are "volunteers." Congressman Rangel is correct though in stating, when he reintroduced his draft proposal in February 2006, that:

> Our military is more like a mercenary force than a citizen militia. It is dominated by men and women who need an economic leg-up. Bonuses of up to $40,000 and a promise of college tuition look very good to someone from an economically depressed urban or rural community.

> ...As the President speaks of a national response involving the military option, military service should be a shared sacrifice. Right now, the only people being asked to sacrifice in any way are those men and women who with limited options, chose military service and now find themselves in harm's way in Iraq. A draft would ensure that every economic group would have to do their share, and not allow some to stay behind while other people's children do the fighting.

> It is shameful for high-ranking government officials who have never placed themselves in harm's way to promote military solutions as a substitute for diplomacy. It's disheartening to hear the most strident champions of war in Iraq or anywhere else who have never thought or voted in Congress to send their own children to war.

I dare anyone to try to convince me that this war is not being fought predominantly by tough, loyal, and patriotic young men and women from the barren hills and towns of rural and underprivileged neighborhoods in urban America where unemployment is high and opportunities are few. As we see who are the troops coming home wounded and killed, I challenge anyone to tell me that the wealthiest have not been excluded from that roll call.

The Federal Government and the Defense Department leadership have become comfortable with the all volunteer force. Secretary Rumsfeld was correct in saying, in understated fashion, that the disadvantages of compulsion were "notable." Senior officers in the military, that remember the draft, dread its return. The all-volunteer force, while creating its own set of challenges, has succeeded in creating a highly professional, career-oriented, motivated force. Many of the behavioral problems associated with inducting, training and employing men who were serving unwillingly, lacking in professionalism and difficult to motivate, have largely become a thing of the past.

While I do not agree with Congressman Rangel's assessment that we have something tantamount to a "mercenary force," I do see problems that neither Congressman Rangel has mentioned nor the Defense Department has admitted to. In a 2006 book, *AWOL The Unexcused Absence of America's Upper Classes from Military Service – and How It Hurts Our Country*, jointly written by Kathy Roth-Douquet and Frank Schaeffer, the disturbing degree to which the more "privileged" among us have avoided military service is exposed. They point out that, unlike in previous times in our history, the sons and daughters of our "upper class" feel no obligation to serve, even in time of war. Expressing concerns similar to Congressman Rangel's, they ask whether leaders who have no military experience or no personal stake in decisions regarding the use of the military force can be trusted to make the right choices on our behalf.

In the past, the children of our most prominent leaders and public figures have served in the military, some in combat. Prominent families, such as the Roosevelts and the Kennedys, had proud histories of military service. The passage from Luke 12:48 that states: "To whom much is given, much is expected" was frequently used as a core reason for the elites of America to serve. Military service was regarded as a "rite of passage" and as a "gateway" to future positions of responsibility and power. Perhaps most familiar to us today is the story of the Kennedy family. Eldest son, Joseph P. Kennedy Jr., and next oldest son, John F. Kennedy, both served on active duty during the Second World War.

Both Kennedys were sons of privilege. Both attended an elite prep school and both attended and graduated from Harvard University. Joseph dropped out of Harvard Law School in order to attend navy pilot training. He was designated a Naval Aviator in May 1942. After completing the requisite number of combat missions, he voluntarily continued his service until he was killed, when the explosives in his aircraft accidentally detonated during a high-risk mission. He was posthumously awarded the Navy Cross, the Distinguished Flying Cross, and the Air Medal. Younger brother, John, also became a naval officer. He, too, served with distinction. His exploits as Commanding Officer of the torpedo patrol boat, PT-109, were prominently chronicled and were instrumental in his election to the presidency in 1960.

The other two Kennedy sons, Robert and Ted, also served in the military. Robert served as an enlisted man in the Navy for a brief period in 1946 and Ted served in the Army from 1951 to 1953. The tradition of military service by America's "royal family" broke down during the next generation. The generation of Joseph Jr. and John failed to pass on the tradition of military service to a collective group of 29 children. While many in the Kennedy family pursued positions of influence and power, none have served in the military.

Kathy Roth-Douquet and Frank Schaeffer also point out the failings of the elite centers of advanced education in sending young men and women into military service. They point out that the Reserve Officer Training Corps (ROTC) program at many civilian universities has withered if not died completely. Prominent private universities, such as Harvard, no longer permit a ROTC program on campus. Princeton, the most elite school with an active ROTC program, is a shadow of its former self. Kathy and Frank point out that in 1956, 400 of the 750 (53 percent) in Princeton's graduating class went into the military while only 9 grads out of roughly 1100 (0.8 percent) entered the military from the Class of 2004.

Another point made in AWOL is of the apparent emergence of a growing "military class." Increasingly, the offspring of military careerists are choosing to follow in the footsteps of one or both of their parents in pursuing military careers of their own. While simplifying the recruiting process, the implications of a military class in a free society is a far cry from the citizens' militia envisioned by the framers of the Constitution. Perhaps most troubling are the reasons that military "legacies" choose the military career path. A sense of isolation from the larger "civilian" society, resulting in a feeling of superiority over it, is among the most common reasons given.

In the end, Kathy and Frank make a similar conclusion to Congressman Rangel's, although for different reasons. Their main premise is that the all-volunteer force, while a professional and proud organization, lacks a proper balance due to the "upper class" of our society taking an almost total "pass" on military service.

The book provides a number of recommendations for resolving the lack of proportionality in the military. Most of the solutions involve some form of a draft or even compulsory service. Kathy's personal preference is to maintain an all-volunteer force but to "invite" members of the upper class to participate. She would appeal to the need and value of "shared sacrifice" as well as applying the same logic employed in earlier times – To whom much is given, much is expected.

Frank's approach is more direct. He proposes that a draft lottery be enacted that would include all young people and that service would not only be limited to the military but would also include civilian service organizations. His plan would leave certain portions of the military, such as the Marine Corps, Navy SEALs, and Army Rangers, in a volunteer status. Undoubtedly under his plan certain people would gravitate toward the volunteer components rather than be drafted into another component that may be felt to be less desirable.

The conclusions made by Congressman Rangel, Kathy Roth-Douquet and Frank Schaeffer are primarily based on class distinctions. Congressman Rangel is most concerned with the "under-class" being over-represented while Kathy and Frank are most concerned with the "upper-class" being under-represented. In both situations the end result is potentially the same. The working class and racial/ethnic minorities are perceived to be suffering the adverse consequences of military service – greater risk of injury or death. The cultural elite, who are also most likely to be in positions of power and decision-making, are perceived to be detached from the negative consequences of war and more prone to make poor decisions and more inclined to promote military "adventurism."

I agree with the general assessments of Congressman Rangel, Kathy Roth-Douquet and Frank Schaeffer; however, recent events in my own life have caused me to question whether the class distinction explanation goes far enough in explaining what is wrong with the all-volunteer force and why an alternative solution, such as a draft, is necessary. I have come to the opinion that the problem is far more corrosive to the concept of "shared sacrifice" than over or under representation of particular classes. I believe that political ideology is rapidly taking over as the major determinant influencing the make-up of our military forces. If current trends continue we are at risk of having a military made up of "Red State" conservatives being directed by "Blue State" liberals.

In 2006, my wife and I, having lived in Rhode Island for sixteen years, decided to relocate in hopes of finding better job opportunities and to live closer to our two children and their spouses, (our daughter was living in southern Virginia and our son was stationed in North Carolina at the time). We targeted North Carolina because it seemed to have some good job opportunities, it was closer to our children, and it appeared to be more "welcoming" to military families like us compared to what we had found in Rhode Island. Our strategy worked. My wife landed a great job as a nurse manager in a county hospital in eastern North Carolina and I had the opportunity to teach at East Carolina University. Even though we thoroughly enjoyed our life and our jobs in North Carolina, after two years my wife decided she wanted new professional challenges in a bigger hospital. We sold our house in North Carolina and packed off for hopefully a new home and new jobs somewhere in New England.

With our recent job experience, we figured finding employment somewhere in New England would be an easy matter. My wife was highly sought after by recruiters specializing in the placement of nurse managers and I was encouraged to apply for a number of municipal management jobs by a consultant specializing in finding town managers and town administrators for New England cities and towns. This particular consultant had very high regard for municipal managers he had known who had prior military experience. He felt that my experience as a career naval officer, my postgraduate education from Harvard, and my prior experience as a municipal manager subsequent to my naval career, qualified me well for the small towns he was representing at the time.

One of the towns that the consultant was representing at the time was my hometown of Westford, Massachusetts. Although Westford was now a bit bigger population-wise than the towns I had been previously associated with, the fact that I was a fourth generation "son" of the town with an extensive knowledge of the town's history and character, the consultant felt I was a "good fit" for the Town Manager position. At the very least, I would get an interview. I applied.

Several weeks passed from the time I submitted my resume and application. Periodically, I would speak with the consultant to get a status report on the review of resumes by the town's search committee and to get some idea when I would need to appear for an interview. Finally, the week came when the consultant was to sit down with the search committee to get their shortlist of applicants to be interviewed. When I called to get the report on the meeting, the consultant, in words of bewilderment, explained that I, and another applicant with a military background, had been rejected, out of hand, because of our military connections. A search committee, with no members with military experience, working for a Board of Selectmen, likewise with no members with military experience, had made it a matter of policy to reject applicants with military backgrounds. How could this happen in a town that so reverently observes Memorial Day each May? How could this happen in a state where the war for independence began? Has political ideology taken root to such an extent that military service is seen as a threat to that ideology?

Although perplexed by the rejection of my hometown, I was inclined to dismiss this incident as an isolated event, until it happened again in two other Massachusetts towns. It became clear to my wife and me that military families such as ours were simply not welcome in an area we had hoped to settle down in and eventually retire. We both gained

131

new insight into how gay members of the military must feel with regard to the "don't ask," don't tell" policy of Congress. We could stay in Massachusetts as long as we didn't say we have a military background. In return, the people of Massachusetts agree not to ask us where we are from.

In attempting to return "home," I learned that the anti-war anti-military sentiments I had observed during my high school years had become institutionalized, not only in my hometown but in the Commonwealth of Massachusetts in general. Since the late 1960s Massachusetts school children and college students had been fed a steady diet of mistrust, if not hatred, for the military. Like a steady diet of sugar resulting in diabetes, the diet of hatred is now manifesting itself in the form of government policy. The school children of the 60s and 70s are now in charge. Regrettably, my generation and the generations that have followed are continuing to ladle out this thick soup of mistrust, resentment and hatred toward the military.

While trying to learn more about the perceived "diversity" problem at the Naval Academy and attempting to prove or refute the claims made by Congressman Rangel, I began digging into various databases to learn more about enlistment trends. I came across one database that showed enlistments by state. I was immediately curious to see how Massachusetts, the state from which I had enlisted in 1970, stacked-up against the other 49 states and the District of Columbia. I learned that Massachusetts was well down the list in terms of active duty recruits. I was also struck by the relatively huge number of recruits coming from Texas. It brought new meaning to the question I got repeatedly from many of the Texan recruits in my boot camp company – "What part of Texas is 'Masatusits' in?"

Recognizing that the report I was looking at was for one year, 2004, I thought perhaps it could be reflecting a one-year anomaly. I decided to go to a more extensive database compiled by the National Priorities Project Database in order to get a broader view of the recruitment picture. What I learned is troubling.

My first step was to compile the active duty recruitment statistics for the Army, Navy, Air Force and Marine Corps for each state. The records for the Army were, by far, the most extensive dating back to the year

2000. In order to avoid short term "blips" in recruitment in individual states, I averaged the recruitments over a five year period of time. Taking an annualized total recruitment for each state, I then calculated the number of active duty recruits per 10,000 males in the population. [Note: The various military recruiting commands use 10,000 enlistment-eligible males for their calculations so while the end numbers may be slightly different the results are proportionately the same.] I then sorted the results from lowest recruitment rate per 10,000 to the highest.

Upon first examination of the resulting list of states and the District of Columbia were not that surprising. There was Texas, second from the top, and there was Massachusetts, fourth from the bottom. On further review however, the results became more stark and disturbing. Of the bottom six states, the states with the relatively lowest contribution to the national defense, four of them were New England states, the other two being the District of Columbia and New Jersey. A trend seemed to be emerging.

Before making any conclusions on the data and keeping in mind the famous quote from Mark Twain about "lies, damn lies, and statistics," I applied a couple of rudimentary statistical measurements. I calculated the Median of the data to be 12.02 recruits per year per 10,000 males in the population. That position was held by the state of Nevada. I then calculated the Standard Deviation. The Standard Deviation allows me to plot the data set against a normal curve in which roughly two-thirds of all data points fall within one Standard Deviation on either side of the Median. The remaining third (33 percent) of the data set will fall on either side of the Median with roughly 16 percent falling well below the Median and 16 percent falling well above the Median. For the purposes of this analysis falling to the right of the Median indicates that these states are contributing more than their fair share of recruits while the states to the left are falling short of their fair share. States falling within the second and third Standard Deviations from the Median are well below or well above their fair shares.

After plotting the Median and the Standard Deviation lines an even more disturbing pattern emerged, especially among the states with, to borrow an oft used Army recruiting term, less "propensity" to enlist. With few exceptions the states to the left of the Median line are in the

Northeast/Mid Atlantic, Upper Midwest, or West Coast. Recalling the Electoral College Maps of the last several presidential elections, I super-imposed the Electoral Vote, "Blue State," "Red State" map onto my data. The results were chilling. For the most recent, 2008 Election, most of the states to the right of the Median line are Red (Republican) and most of the states to the left are Blue (Democrat). The results are even starker for the more closely contested elections of 2000 and 2004. When these elections are applied, virtually the entire right side of the graph is Red as well as the upper half of the first Standard Deviation to the left of the Median.

As noted, there are a few states that defy my initial conclusion that there is a relationship between the predominant political ideology within a state and that state's national military participation. I sought to get a deeper understanding of why a state might depart from the pre-dicted outcome by contacting the Army recruiting commands respon-sible for the recruiting programs in the "outlier" states. In each case, I was told that the Army has not and does not analyze recruitment on the basis I was using; therefore, they were initially reluctant to comment. However, when I explained I was more interested in "gut feelings" rather than statistical analysis, the Army's regional experts were more forth-coming and enlightening.

My first question had to do with North Dakota. North Dakota is a "Red" state that falls below the First Standard Deviation. How can this state's low recruitment rate be explained? Why is North Dakota different from South Dakota? Why is it only slightly better than its "Blue" neigh-bor, Minnesota? The immediate answer was: "low unemployment." The unemployment rate in North Dakota is currently around 3 percent, well below the national average. The reason given by the Army for the high employment of potential recruits in North Dakota is the rapid recent growth of the "energy economy" due to recent discovery of oil and natu-ral gas deposits within the state. (This explanation tends to confirm the claim made by Congressman Rangel that recruitment is largely driven by economic status).

Utah was another "Red" state that does not fit the initial assump-tions. The Army recruiters could not help me other than to say that the Coast Guard gets a disproportionate number of volunteers from Utah. My personal theory regarding Utah stems from the fact that Utah's

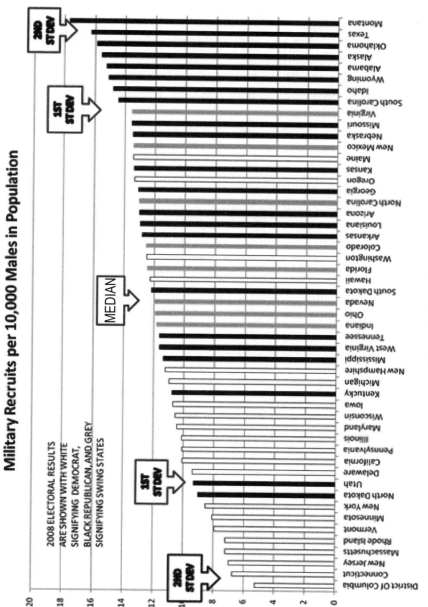

Military Recruits per 10,000 Males in Population

2008 ELECTORAL RESULTS
ARE SHOWN WITH WHITE
SIGNIFYING DEMOCRAT,
BLACK REPUBLICAN, AND GREY
SIGNIFYING SWING STATES

50 States plus District of Columbia

population is nearly 70 percent Mormon. The Mormon religion has a "missionary" program in which young men between the ages of 19 and 21 are expected to devote a two year period of their lives to missionary work and service. Since this age group is also the prime age group for military enlistment, I would surmise that most of these young men forgo military service in order to answer the calling of their church.

Although not as stark a difference as North Dakota and Utah on the left side of the Median line, there are three "Blue" states that defy a simple explanation – Maine, Oregon and Washington. Maine has become a reliably "Blue" state in presidential elections, yet its military recruitment is nearly at the opposite end of the curve from its sister New England states, including the "Live Free or Die" state, New Hampshire. According to an Army recruiting expert with extensive experience in the Northeast, Maine, perhaps more than any of its sister states, retains many of its "rural traditions," including national military service. Maine, until recently, had more of an active duty military presence than the other New England states. A military presence in a region can often translate into a greater regional acceptance of the military culture. Furthermore, an active duty military presence also translates into a greater likelihood of military retirees settling in that region. As Kathy and Frank pointed out in AWOL, military retirees "spawn" military recruits. The Army expert also points out job opportunities for young men in Maine are scarce.

Oregon and Washington do not fit neatly into my theory. The Army could provide no answer for why Oregon and Washington are at the opposite end of the chart from their big neighbor to the south, California. I suspect there is a combination of many factors at work in these two reliably "Blue" states in the Pacific Northwest. Poor economy in parts of Oregon, traditionally associated with logging; rural traditions, like in Maine, and strong regional active duty military presenc, may all contribute to a higher than expected military participation.

Anyone who has taken a statistics class in college can tell you that one has to be cautious about concluding that a correlation of data means there is a causal relationship. In this case; however, there is strong evidence to suggest that political ideologies within geographic regions, within media market areas, and within individual states, have a strong impact upon military recruitment.

Economics and unemployment are the "usual suspects" when explaining variations in recruiting; however, these explanations quickly melt away when one considers two states with the worst unemployment, Michigan and Rhode Island. Ranked #1 and #2 respectively in worst unemployment, Michigan and Rhode Island are among the states with the weakest support for the military. Another excuse given for lack of military participation is "proximity to active duty forces." Until recently, the U.S. Navy was the number one employer in the state of Rhode Island. The Navy still maintains a high profile in the state. Yet, Rhode Island is among the most military "unfriendly" states and fifth from the bottom in terms of military participation. As a recent, sixteen year, resident of Rhode Island, I am convinced that a "political ideology" hostile to military service is the predominant reason for Rhode Island's poor showing. Having grown up in Massachusetts and having more recently listened to the anti-military classroom vitriol as a graduate student at Harvard, I am equally convinced that Massachusetts suffers from the same mutation of political ideology.

This mutation of our political discourse is not isolated to the Northeast and Mid Atlantic. The West Coast variant of the anti-military "virus" that discourages participation in the military is perhaps best exemplified by the City by the Bay – San Francisco.

During the mid-1980s, my family and I lived in San Francisco when I was assigned to the aircraft carrier, Enterprise. Our homeport was in nearby Alameda. San Francisco is among the most beautiful cities in the world. My wife and I enjoyed our time there so much we often said at the time that if we could choose but one place to live in the world, it would be San Francisco. When I served in Enterprise the San Francisco Bay Area was home to several major military facilities besides two nuclear aircraft carriers and two nuclear cruisers. In addition to the naval air station and seaport at Alameda, other facilities such as the Oakland Army Base, the Oak Knoll Naval Hospital, and the Presidio Army base, supported a huge active duty presence in the northern California region.

Few cities in the United States enjoy the high place of honor in our military history as San Francisco does. San Francisco came into its own as a hub of military activity during the Second World War. Many a farewell toast was raised at the "Top of the Mark" (Hopkins Hotel), by men about to depart for war action somewhere in the Pacific theater of operations. Unfortunately, beginning in the mid-1980s, as the Navy attempted to grow to a strength of 600 ships, the Bay Area's history of radical opposition to the Viet Nam War converged with the post-Viet Nam military. The "protesters" of the 60s and early 70s seized on the opportunity to "suit up" for another fight, this time to block the strategic homeporting of the battleship Missouri in San Francisco. They succeeded in blocking the battleship and at the same time, set in motion a process that would lead to the demise of the Bay Area as a friendly home for the military. Within five years all major military facilities in the Bay Area closed.

The complete loss of the military presence was not enough for some. In recent years, San Francisco has blocked attempts to create a museum and memorial centered on the decommissioned battleship, Iowa. Votes have been taken to end Junior ROTC programs from public high schools. Attempts have been made to expel local military recruiting offices. The Marine Corps was forbidden from filming a recruiting video on a city street.

The excuse, in virtually all cases, has been linked to San Francisco's official opposition to the "Don't Ask, Don't Tell" policy of the Congress regarding gays, lesbians and transgender people serving in the military. San Francisco has become center-stage to a political ideology that is overtly and unapologetically pro-gay rights and anti-military. The proponents of this ideology have been successful in presenting San Francisco's opposition as the "template" upon which other regions of California and of the country can build. Even more ominously, the political ideology espoused by San Francisco has become intertwined with the ideology of the Democratic Party.

A symbiotic relationship has developed between the political ideology of the Democratic Party and the ideology of mistrust and hate toward the military. As the results of recent presidential elections show, the Democratic Party is highly dependent on the votes coming from the highly populated regions of the Northeast, Mid Atlantic Coast, Upper Midwest, and the West Coast. Presidential politics has become one of Electoral Vote counting rather than of what is best for the nation as a whole. Our two political parties have ceded entire regions to the other. As a result, the margins of victory for presidential candidates have been decided by the voting in just a few "swing states" that have yet to identify themselves as either reliably Democrat or reliably Republican. A party's unwillingness, or inability, to contest elections in every state serves only to reinforce the prevailing dominant political ideology in that state. An uncontested California, with its huge treasure of Electoral College votes, will lead to only a deeper and deeper ideological divide as well as stronger and stronger animus toward the military.

Our military, by nature, is and should be an apolitical entity, beholden to neither political party. If this apparent trend toward parallel political polarization of military recruitment based on political ideology continues, we may arrive at a time where our military is faced with the untenable position of being deeply rooted in one political party yet controlled by the other. The consequences of such a condition threaten our very existence as a republic.

A situation in which the majority of our military come from conservative leaning, Republican voting, rural living, regions of the county is unacceptable for both political parties. One can envision this trend culminating in one of several conditions that would make the United States both vulnerable to collapse from within or to conquest by an outside force.

The spectrum of possible consequences range from the opposite extremes of - the decline of military capability due to benign neglect accompanied by mass voluntary separation by the most skilled warriors; to the unthinkable "Seven Days in May" scenario of a military challenge to civilian control in which the military acts in its own self interest for the perceived good of the country. The prospect of a military dominated by one political ideology being directed by the opposing ideology presents a veritable "minefield" of dire consequences. As alluded to by Congressman Rangel in his various proposals to reinstate the draft, we do not want a detached civilian leadership with no military experience. We do not want an elite governing class, with no personal stake in military action, directing the actions of a military force made up of men and women that do not represent a cross section of the society from which they come. Unlike Congressman Rangel's vision though, instead of a force that is racially and economically unbalanced, I foresee a situation that is even more injurious to our national goals and core principles – a military force that neither trusts its leaders nor understands what it is fighting for.

139

Where To From Here

The purpose of this book has been to illuminate four specific areas of United States national policy that are detrimental to the conduct of armed conflict. Books of this type would not be complete without the author ascending his or her soapbox to loudly proclaim these faults and with equal volume explain how the problem should be solved. As I ascend to my soapbox I will simply preface my remarks by saying that my recommendations are intended to be based on common sense as well as the lessons of history.

I bring to my recommendations a perspective based largely on my experience as a career naval officer; as a student, teacher and practitioner of government; and as the father and father-in-law of active duty military officers. My views are both professional and personal.

In this book I have identified and illustrated four major problem areas that I feel hamper the effectiveness of the military, and by extension, the policies of the United States:

(1) Since the Second World War, the American People have been effectively left out of the decision-making process when considering when to fight, where to fight, and whether to fight a war. Failing to include the people has resulted in the eventual loss of support for a military effort that the national government has entered into on behalf of the American people. Loss of public support has led to loss of support within the very government that initially entered into the conflict. The result has been indecisive outcomes, needless expenditure of blood and treasure, and, at times, defeat. None of these outcomes are acceptable

(2) Since the Second World War, the United States has engaged in "limited wars." In virtually all cases the circumstances under which armed forces have been committed

have not been appropriate for the "limited form" of warfare. The failure to recognize this fact has resulted in conflicts with indecisive outcomes, needless expenditure of blood and treasure and, at times, defeat. Recognition by the national government that only "unlimited" warfare was appropriate to the situation could have resulted in an earlier, less costly victory, or, a decision to pursue other options short of armed intervention in the first place.

(3) Since the Second World War, the United States has not "declared war" in accordance with the Constitution. Rather, the national government has entered into armed conflicts with the "authorization" of Congress. The authorization process was formalized in 1973 by the enactment, over presidential veto, of the War Powers Resolution. The War Powers Resolution has enabled Congress to give only half-hearted, tentative, and easily retractable support in carrying out what should be the national government's most solemn duty – the commitment of troops to combat. The War Powers Resolution has provided the Congress with the necessary "wiggle words" and "trap doors" with which to escape accountability for its actions relative to fighting war. The War Powers Resolution has intentionally encumbered the president in carrying out the president's Constitutional role of Commander in Chief of the armed forces. The loss of Congressional support subsequent to initial enthusiastic support has contributed to loss of troop morale, indecisive outcomes, needless expenditure of blood and treasure and, at times, defeat.

(4) Finally, during the Viet Nam War, Congress and the President grossly mismanaged the selective service system. A maze of inequitable draft deferments concocted by the Congress led to a condition of near anarchy within the United States. In response to the outcry against the draft

and against the protracted military involvement in Southeast Asia, Congress and the President ended the draft and established an All-Volunteer Force. In response to other prevailing social issues at the time of the creation of the all-volunteer military, the Congress has repeatedly imposed social changes onto the military that it was unable to impose onto the population at large. Though perhaps with the best of intentions, the imposition of "social experiments" onto the military has resulted in the unintended consequence of a force not totally focused on what should be its one and only goal – be prepared to fight and win wars decisively, expeditiously, and with the minimum loss of blood and treasure.

These are the four fundamental problem areas that I feel have hampered and continue to hamper the United States since the Second World War. As the result of the outcome of the Second World War the United States, for the first time in its history, assumed a role as a world power. For the first time in its history, the United States has maintained a large and well equipped standing armed force. And, for the first time in its history, the United States has repeatedly engaged in undeclared expeditionary wars. The United States has chosen to maintain its position as a preeminent world power using a large standing armed force made up of volunteers.

I believe that the United States, while navigating through uncharted waters, has made some wrong turns since the conclusion of the Second World War. I believe that it is not too late to change course. The most sacred purpose of the national government is to provide for the "common defense." All other purposes are subordinate to this trust for without security no other purpose can long survive.

We the People at War

Clausewitz explained many things about war. He distilled the nature of war into three essential elements commonly referred to as the "trinity" of war. Of the three elements, the "people" have been reduced to bystander status since the Second World War. Our presidents, our representatives and our senators have intentionally marginalized the role the people play in fighting our wars, except, of course, for taking their sons and daughters to engage in the fight. The people have been marginalized out of either a misplaced desire to avoid "imposing" on the people, or, to prevent the people from participating in the decision-making process. In all too many cases, our senators and representatives have assumed roles as "rulers" rather than as "representatives."

I suspect the marginalization of the people was, at first, with the best of intentions. The Second World War was still fresh in the memories of the people when Korea erupted. The people were "war weary" after all. The people had been asked to sacrifice a lot. Surely, a small peninsula on the other side of the world would be a momentary distraction compared to the global scope of the Second World War. Asking the people to sacrifice for the Korean War was viewed as, not only too much for the people to bear, so soon after the global war. Furthermore, sacrifice on the scope of that of the Second World War was simply unnecessary. The new status and wealth enjoyed by the United States meant we now had the luxury of not having to choose between "guns or butter." We could have both.

Korea was still not completely removed from the consciousness of the people. The draft remained, even after the cease fire was achieved in 1951. Most draft eligible young men still had the expectation of serving at some time either following high school or beginning in college as part of the ROTC program. The marginalization of the people and their role in war became fully institutionalized during the Viet Nam War as President Johnson aggressively pursued an agenda in which we could fight a foreign war while at the same time create new, ambitious and costly domestic programs such as the "The Great Society" and "Medicare." Apparently, we could not only have "guns and butter" we could also have our "cake and eat it, too."

In Viet Nam, the side benefit of keeping the people in the dark, permitted the Congress to get by with passing the Tonkin Gulf Resolution in lieu of declaring war. The Tonkin Gulf Incident never achieved the outcry from the people to avenge the supposed attack on our naval forces in the South China Sea the same way that Japan's attack on our naval forces in Pearl Harbor had. Congress successfully demonstrated that the United States could enter into a major war without major debate and without consultation with the people. It completely escaped the Congress and the President that the sacrifices made by the people during the Second World War were in fact critical elements of a winning war strategy. Sacrifice in their daily lives had caused the people to be a part of the war effort.

Other than through the direct participation in a war effort through military service, participation in war by the people needs to become an integral part of the national government's war strategy. Inclusion of the people should be of equal importance to matters such as providing for the material support of our troops in a war zone. Each American should be reminded daily of the sacrifices of our soldiers, sailors, airmen and marines through meaningful as well as symbolic sacrifices in their own daily lives.

During the Second World War, the people were involved with the war effort through measures such as rationing and air raid watches. Even though rationing was used as a conservation measure to ensure an adequate supply of strategically important materials, it was also a regular and tangible inconvenience that served to remind the people that it was not "business as usual." Rationing went beyond the simple rules of supply and demand. Rationing provided a limit to how much of a quantity could be consumed. It was not a matter of simply paying a few more cents. Everyone, rich and poor, was affected by the daily inconveniences caused by rationing.

The need to preserve raw materials and commodities to directly support the combat forces is greatly diminished in comparison to the need during the Second World War. This change is largely due to the much smaller size of the military being supported. Today's force is a small fraction of the size of the total force assembled during the Second World War. Nevertheless, there are still sacrifices that can be made that have both meaning and substance.

Creating a sense of shared sacrifice will require imagination and innovation, not just a new tax or surcharge. Shared sacrifice is more than sticking an "I support the troops" yellow ribbon magnet on the rear hatch to our SUVs. Shared sacrifice is more than a flag lapel pin. Shared sacrifice is not singing "God Bless America" during the seventh inning stretch. Shared sacrifice is not cheering an F-18 Hornet fly-over before kickoff. Shared sacrifice needs to be something that impacts our daily lives and reminds us that there are troops fighting on our behalf who don't get a full night's sleep in a comfortable bed; who don't get to bathe and shampoo in a hot shower; who don't get to sit down to dinner with loved ones.

Limited War

As explained previously in this book, the United States has engaged in several "limited wars" since the end of the Second World War. In each case the criteria for limited war, as defined by British naval historian, Julian S. Corbett, has not been met. In each case the cost in terms of blood and treasure has been substantial. And, in each case thus far, the results have been something short of decisive victory. The Korean War resulted in a ceasefire that has tenuously held for more than fifty years. The Viet Nam War resulted in defeat on the battlefield and a longstanding division of the United States over the use of military force. The First Iraq War resulted in more than ten years of continued flaunting of United Nations mandates by Iraq. The Second Iraq War has continued for longer than any previous war in American history. It remains to be seen if the objective of establishing a lasting democratic government in the Middle East will succeed. The War in Afghanistan is following in similar fashion to three previous wars involving the British and the more recent war involving the Soviet Union. There is no assurance that the United States will succeed against essentially the same enemy that soundly defeated the British and the Soviets.

In every attempt thus far at limited war, the United States has failed to satisfy the most basic of prerequisites for limited war to succeed – strategic isolation of the territorial objective. In no case has the United States succeeded in taking the regions contiguous with the territorial objective out of the fight completely. In each case, this failure has been the direct cause of achieving something less than decisive victory. In Viet Nam it caused defeat.

The United States, in weighing whether or not to use military force to achieve its policy objectives, has two questions to answer.

(1)   Does the territorial object of this proposed use of military force <u>completely</u> fit the criteria for limited warfare? Yes or No.

(2)   If the answer is "no," is the United States prepared to use "unlimited" means in order to achieve its objectives? Yes or No

In each case since the Second World War, the answer to both questions has been "no." Since the United States has been either unwilling or unprepared to resort to unlimited means, then other methods, short of military force, should have been employed. If and when those "other methods" fail the United States is faced anew with decision-point #2 – is the United States prepared to use "unlimited" means? Except in the rare case of an extremely limited objective, the "limited" option will never materialize unless the criteria for the limited option are fully met.

This apparent dilemma does not preclude the use of unlimited means; however, this situation will by necessity force the "trinity" of war – the government, the military and the people – to enter into a dialogue to determine if: (1) the proposed cause of war is in the national interest; (2) the objective is militarily practicable with the current force strength; (3) the war is sustainable over a long term; and, (4) the benefits of the war outweigh the projected costs in terms of blood and treasure. A period of dialogue would force us to ask the difficult questions that need answers prior to the first shot being fired.

Had questions relative to the characterization of objectives being either "limited" or "unlimited" been asked prior to entering into the various major armed conflicts subsequent to the Second World War, the course of history would have been much different. Failure to ask the hard questions has had lasting negative consequences.

Had we concluded to fight the Korean War in an unlimited manner it is possible, if not likely, that the Cold War could have been avoided; the rise of Communist China could have been checked during its infancy; the conditions that brought about the Viet Nam War never would have arisen; the proliferation of nuclear weapons could have been prevented; the ambiguous ceasefire and the suffering of the North Korean people of the last 50 years would have been avoided; the spread of communism in the Soviet sphere of influence likely could have been stemmed.

Had we concluded that the Viet Nam War could not be fought in a limited fashion, we would have recognized that the opportunity to stem the spread of communism was Korea, not Southeast Asia, and that while well intentioned, a ground war in Southeast Asia was folly.

Had we concluded that the Second Iraq War could not be fought without taking into account Iraq's contiguous neighbors, the war could have been dramatically shortened by dramatically stemming the tide of "foreign fighters" and explosive devises flowing into the country from Syria and Iran.

Had we reviewed the history of failure of outside forces fighting in the desert and mountain terrain of Afghanistan, I doubt that we would have committed any conventional ground forces to the area at all. A review of Afghanistan's history also might have revealed other means to achieve our objectives. Certainly a fair assessment of Afghanistan's plight can be traced to the British administration of the region beginning in the 19th Century. Most of our current problems with Afghanistan are the creations of the West and in particular our closest ally, Great Britain. It seems to me that true and lasting negotiated solutions need to be brokered by Britain, not the United States. Perhaps most importantly, Britain and the United States need to recognize and deal honestly with the corrosive role that Pakistan plays in the Afghanistan problem. Without Pakistan's full cooperation, including territorial concessions, no lasting resolution can be achieved for Afghanistan. Bottom line – Afghanistan is no place for a war, limited or unlimited.

As a way of better comprehending and following what I have called "Corbett's Rules," I have included a simple checklist to quickly assess the worthiness of what might be regarded as a "limited objective" for war. I recommend that the checklist be cut-out and taped into the binder of each Congressman's and each Senator's pocket Constitution. The United States should never again enter into an "unlimited war" in a "limited" way.

147

UNITED STATES			OBJECT TERRITORY		
CONSTANTS	Y	N	CONSTANTS	Y	N
Island Power			Remote Location		
Command of the Seas			Command of the Seas		
			Sea Girt		
VARIABLES			VARIABLES		
Limited Object			Limited Object		
Popular Repugnance			Antagonistic Behavior		
			Strategic Isolation		

The Corbett Test
(Cut along dotted line)

In considering future use of military force in which the "object territory" fails the Corbett Test, what should the Congress and President consider when weighing the unlimited option?

Aside from the absence of a limited object and an inability to strategically isolate the object, the unlimited option is similar to the limited option in that command of the seas must be maintained and the homeland must remain protected. Furthermore, the object territory needs to have exhibited an "antagonistic behavior" that engenders a "popular repugnance" among the American people sufficient to warrant going to war.

The unlimited option however goes beyond the limited option in terms of the size and degree of force employed to achieve total and absolute victory. The unlimited option means that "all options are on the table." The ramifications of unlimited war that must be considered by the government, the military and the people are extensive. Some examples of the types of consideration to be faced are:

- States that are contiguous to the primary object territory.
- Reaction of rival interests such as those of Russian and China.
- Conditions under which nuclear weapons will be used.

- Non-military and civilian targets to be pursued.
- How many men will be drafted?
- Will women be drafted?

A brief glimpse into the "Pandora's Box," opened by entering into an unlimited use of military force, tells us why the United States Congress and our presidents prefer to convince themselves that "the next war will be different" rather than confronting the cold hard realities of the limited option. Aided and abetted by a military constrained by its allegiance to civilian leadership; bridled by its ever-present "can do" spirit; and led by generals and admirals that are more at home in Washington than they are in the field or at sea, the government has repeatedly embarked on foreign expeditions that aptly fit Einstein's definition of insanity – "doing the same thing over and over and expecting different results."

War Powers

As pointed out earlier in the book, Congress has sidestepped its obligations under the Constitution by supplanting the "declaration of war" with the worm-like practice of "statutory authorization." Starting with the Tonkin Gulf Resolution and formalized in the War Powers Resolution of 1973, Congress has created an expansion of its Constitutional powers. As a result, contrary to the unmatched wisdom of our nation's founders, Congress has established a policy of "leadership by committee."

Congressional action under the War Powers Resolution subsequent to its passage in 1973, has been marked by political partisanship rather than wisdom. The War Powers Resolution has provided Congress with an avenue of easy escape when public opinion wavers. War strategy is now driven more by polls and election cycles than by sound and steady judgment.

The War Powers Resolution was purportedly created in response to a change in United States post-war behavior. Members of Congress reasoned that by retaining a large standing army during peacetime, the President would be tempted to abuse his powers as Commander in Chief.

Four years after unanimously approving a presidential response to Iraq's defiance of the United Nations, Congress revisited the issue of Iraq. The conditions in Iraq had only gotten worse and they were exacerbated by the events of September 11ᵗʰ 2001. Nevertheless, the response by the Senate was quite different. While the make-up of the Senate had changed little in those four years, President Clinton had left office and was replaced by Republican, George Bush. At a time when unanimous consent would have signaled strong national resolve, the senate split its vote largely on political party lines.

The Democrat senator's true intentions were further illuminated by a failed resolution that held out an option for a future "declaration of war" in lieu of a statutory authorization. This legislation and the comments made by several Democrat senators subsequent to the legislation showed that they clearly understood the distinction between a "declared" war and an "authorized" war. Clearly, the senators preferred the "authorized" war method as means of retaining greater power for themselves while depriving a Republican president of his full Constitutional powers. The split vote on statutory authorization also enabled Democrat senators who had voted in favor of armed force to renege on their votes within a year.

The rapid turnabout by certain Democrat senators was clearly taken for political advantage in the lead-up to the 2004 Presidential Election. Democrat candidates for president sought to be identified as the most "authentic" anti-war candidate. While failing to get a Democrat elected to the presidency in 2004 the tone set by the anti-war strategy succeeded in leading public opinion on the war downward during a critical point in the war. The campaign of 2004 set the stage for the 2006 mid-term election and the 2008 Presidential Election. 2004 Vice Presidential candidate, John Edwards, authored the "template" for the 2008 Election less than one year after the 2004 election, based solely on his renunciation of his prior vote to authorize military force in Iraq.

The time to debate war is prior to the commitment of armed forces to the battlefield, not after. When a Congress decides to commit armed force to battle it should be incumbent on the entire government, not just the president, to support the war effort. When a government sends an armed force to war, every effort should be taken to both support the armed forces as well as sustain the public support necessary to successfully prosecute that war. To the greatest degree possible, politics should be removed from the use of armed force. This can best be achieved by treating the initial decision to go to war as a solemn and apolitical act of government.

The War Powers Resolution should be repealed. All future wars should be declared in accordance with the Constitution. The act of declaring war will better ensure that the use of military force is not entered into capriciously. The act of declaring war will better ensure an unwavering, solemn commitment to victory by the government, the military and the people.

Eye on the Ball

"Social Engineering" by the Congress has seriously undermined military readiness. The military's ability to fight and win wars has been subordinated to the career competitiveness of women as well as the racial, ethnic and sexual identities of soldiers, sailors, airmen and marines. The "All-Volunteer Force" has evolved into a military that no longer resembles a cross-section of America in terms of race, ethnicity and economic class. State and regional political ideology is becoming the primary determinant in regional representation within the military.

Getting our "eye" back "on the ball" is critical to our national security. The government, the military and the people need to refocus on the purpose of having an armed force – being prepared to fight and win wars. Similar to building a winning football team, our national policy should be to assemble the best possible military team with the best chance of being victorious. The aspects of gender, race, ethnicity and sexual orientation should be subordinated, if not totally discounted, in the pursuit of this goal.

The make-up of the military, each of its service components, each military unit, and each military member should be determined by how best to attain the goal of assembling the strongest team with the greatest likelihood of victory.

For the military, there should be a single standard of achieving a balanced force that resembles the broad cross-section of the general population. Each state should contribute a proportionate number of people to the military services based on each state's population. The prescribed size (end strength) of the military should determine the total number of military members from each state per military component. This is to prevent a small number of states dominating the make-up of one particular service component, i.e. Army, Navy, Air Force, Marine Corps.

Proportional representation is not unprecedented in the United States. The principle is enshrined in Article I Section 2 of the Constitution. It prescribes the method by which Representatives are assigned. Proportionality is periodically adjusted by means of enumeration of the nation's population, commonly referred to as a decennial census. The make-up of the military service academies is determined by proportional representation based on state population. Seemingly, a similar method for managing military recruitment and a supplemental military draft would not present too steep of a mountain to climb. Unlike current recruiting programs, such as the Naval Academy's "diversity" program, a proportional recruitment/draft selective service program would certainly pass constitutional muster.

A partial, or supplemental military draft would enable us to retain the most positive aspects of having an all volunteer force, while at the same time, control costs and help to resolve some of the real, and perceived inequities that have arisen since the demise of the national draft. A supplemental draft system would enable the military to "flex" in size during times of peace as well as national emergencies. A supplemental draft would better enable the military to recruit high quality without sacrificing principles of demographic proportionality, as well as racial and ethnic diversity.

For states that fail to attain their prescribed proportional representation through voluntary enlistment, a state-wide, no deferment, draft lottery should be held in order to attain the prescribed level of participation. Draftees would have the option of volunteering for a regular four-year enlistment where individual service and job preference desires would be considered. Draftees not desiring to take-on a four-year commitment would be inducted into a two-year program with no consideration for

152

personal preference for service component or job classification. By necessity, a majority of two-year draftees would be inducted into the lower skill/higher population segments of the services. The Army, being the largest of the armed services, would be the predominant destination for two-year draftees.

A minimum period of two years of military service should be required as a "gateway" to various federal programs. For example, military service should be a prerequisite for any civilian employment by the federal government, e.g. congressional staff members and department employees.

There should be a single minimum acceptable standard for all service men and women. Eligibility for service should be determined by measurable mental and physical standards. Due to wide variations in education standards among the various states, minimum competency would be assessed by standardized tests. Minimum mental and physical standards should be attained by both volunteers and draftees. Failure to achieve eligibility for military service would result in forfeiture of eligibility for certain federal programs such as guaranteed college student loans.

For the individual service components, there should be service-unique requirements related to the needs of the particular component. Each occupational area within each service should have its own standards and qualification requirements. To the greatest extent possible, where licensure standards exist for military occupation areas, the initial attainment of and maintenance of those standards should be required in addition to attainment and maintenance of service component standards and qualifications. This measure is necessary to ensure uniform standards service-wide. This measure also has a side benefit of qualifying service members for non-military applications of their skills gained through their military service. For example, military pilots are required to hold a Federal Aviation Administration license. Military pilots are required to meet both FAA minimum standards as well as fulfilling the standards unique to their individual services or aircraft types. On the other hand, naval officers serving aboard surface ships have no licensure requirements even though there are federal and international licensure standards for all officers serving aboard non-military seagoing vessels.

Licensure of surface ship officers is one issue that should be resolved sooner rather than later.

The use of uniform and universally accepted standards for military occupations necessitates that the military recruit people that can attain these standards. The use of two-tiered qualification standards, such as those being employed at the Naval Academy to achieve "diversity," is contrary to the goal of recruiting the best possible military "team," a team that is prepared to fight and win wars, not games.

An assessment should be conducted of each military unit relative to the considerations of gender, race, ethnicity, and sexual orientation. The unit's ability to accomplish its assigned mission should be the sole determinant in deciding whether or not women are intentionally assigned; and, whether or not openly gay personnel are intentionally assigned. The only assessment regarding race and ethnicity should be that there is no consideration based on race or ethnicity. Qualification standards should be colorblind. Affirmative action in the military is as detrimental to the individual minority service member as it is to the mission readiness of the service component in which they serve.

Regarding the role of women in the military, there are military units in which women are distinct enhancements to mission readiness while in other units they are distinct distractions to mission readiness, even in those units where the women are otherwise fully qualified. In those cases where mission readiness is either neutrally or positively affected by the presence of women, then women should be assigned to units of that type or class. However, in cases where mission readiness is negatively affected by the presence of women, then women should not be assigned to units of that type or class.

The first question that comes to mind regarding the assignment of women is: How do you objectively determine whether or not the presence of women is detrimental to mission readiness? The answer lies in the answer to one of the next two questions:

(1)   Has the unit's mission readiness been adversely and un reasonably affected by behavioral infractions stemming from male/female relations?

(2)   Has the unit's mission readiness been adversely and un-

reasonably affected by the accommodations that must be made for women who become pregnant?

If the answer to either of these questions is "yes," then women should not be assigned to units of that type or class. Mission readiness is not about fairness, it is about being prepared to fight and win wars.

A policy of placing mission readiness at the center of personnel assignments will deprive women of opportunities to serve in units that are most likely to engage in combat operations. Barring women from certain types and classes of military units will have an adverse affect on promotion opportunities for women. Again, mission readiness is not about fairness, it is about being prepared to fight and win wars.

Military service and combat operations, by nature, are asexual. Open sexuality, heterosexual or homosexual, is detrimental to virtually any workplace. Open sexuality is especially detrimental to the "good order and discipline" required in combat capable military units. Open homosexuality is as detrimental to unit cohesion as open heterosexuality is. The same reasons that women should not serve in particular military units, made up predominantly of young, straight men, apply to gay, lesbian and transgender people.

With this in mind, let it be said that, gay, lesbian and transgender people have served, do serve, and will continue to serve with honor in the military. The movement to permit openly gay, lesbian and transgender people to serve is an ideologically motivated smokescreen designed to promote a political agenda and encourage continued social experimentation by Congress.

Admittedly gay, lesbian and transgender people should be permitted to serve in the military. Openly homosexual behavior in the military should be prohibited as should openly heterosexual behavior. Any behavior of a sexual nature should not be tolerated in the confines of any military unit or installation. People who self-identify themselves as gay, lesbian or transgender should be assigned in similar fashion to women. If the presence of a gay, lesbian or transgender people negatively affect a unit's mission readiness, they should not be assigned to that unit. If the presence of gay, lesbian or transgender people neutrally or positively affect a unit's mission readiness, they should be assigned to that unit.

155

There are many challenging and rewarding jobs within the military services that can readily accommodate straight women, gay men, lesbians and transgender people without compromising mission readiness. Congress and the President should refocus national policy on achieving and maintaining maximum mission readiness. A commitment to this single, central and incontrovertible principle of war will serve us well as a nation and as a people.

Epilogue

When I began writing this book, I had several preconceived notions about what I expected to find and what I expected to conclude. As I mentioned earlier, I was drawn to this project when I began my reading to prepare to teach a course on war. My excursion into Clausewitz had helped me explain my curiosity with the "war stories" I had heard as a child. Not until reading Clausewitz and contemplating his "trinity theory," had I understood the pivotal role that "we the people" play in war. I had intended to write a book purely on the central role that "we the people" played in achieving victory in the Second World War and how our failure to include "we the people" in war subsequent to that victory had led to less than conclusive results, certainly not victories.

Along the way, I learned that our failure to achieve clear and conclusive results was a bit more complicated. It was not enough to say if we had included the people in the equation the results would have been different. There were other elements involved that have led to unnecessarily entering into armed conflicts. Likewise, there were other elements that led to failed attempts to achieve clear and conclusive victories with a minimum loss of blood and treasure.

By applying Sir Julian Corbett's reasoning for how the British Empire succeeded to the United States' attempts at limited war, I came to the conclusion that none of the armed conflicts entered into by the United States since the Second World War fit Corbett's definition of limited war. Corbett's expansion on the theories of limited war, first put forth by Clausewitz, help to explain why we failed in Korea and Viet Nam and why our efforts in Iraq and Afghanistan are ultimately likely to fail. While it can be argued that Corbett's definition of limited war is simply theoretical, I think history of the last sixty years provides adequate proof that his definition is indeed fact.

It is counterintuitive to accept Corbett's findings as fact. How can an explanation of limited war be so simple, yet so right? Surely, the United States, the world's greatest and last super power, can achieve victory by simply applying a bit more force; by committing a few more troops; by dropping a few more bombs; or, by spending a bit more money. It was a bitter pill for me to swallow as a former career naval officer that the wars of my lifetime were entered erroneously. This is not to say that these wars have been entered into without the best of intentions. This is not to say that these wars should not have been fought at all. What it does say, though, is that none of them could have been fought in a limited way.

The exploration of the limited war fallacy led me to seek accountability. Who or what was responsible for steering us the wrong direction after achieving such apparent success in the Second World War? While there are many people and many individual decisions that can be pointed to in assessing our "track record," I believe that our failures are rooted in the decision to not seek a formal declaration of war in Korea. Undoubtedly, historians and politicians can argue the justifications for not declaring war in Korea; however, the precedent set by the government at that time, lives with us to this day. The double failure to recognize that the Korean War could not be fought in a limited way and that it was somehow not worthy of a formal declaration of war by Congress, set us on a slippery slope to where we are today – doing the same thing repeatedly and expecting different results.

While compiling this book, several things have surprised me. I have veered in directions I had not anticipated and I arrived at conclusions I could not have predicted. Some of these surprises have caused me to change the way I look at the use of armed force while others have caused me to rethink national policies seemingly remote from the subject of war and the topic of this book. The comments to follow are devoted to summarizing these surprises.

War Powers Act, the President and the Congress

As a military professional, I was taught to leave my political philosophy "on the beach." It was ingrained in me from the time I took my first oath on the 19th of November 1970, that our civilian government would decide when, where, and how to employ my services. I believed that in return for my allegiance to my oath that the government would do its best to make the right decisions, equally unencumbered by political philosophy. I guess my somewhat naïve view of military service came from my earliest recollections from hearing my parents, aunts, uncles and grandparents talk of the experience of the Second World War. I had assumed that the behavior of the government during that war would directly transfer to the wars of my lifetime.

I had expected that the War Powers Resolution of 1973 would prove to be a way for legislators to sidestep their Constitutional responsibility to deliberate and decide on whether or not to declare war. I had expected that the "statutory authorization" that would take the place of formal declarations of war would enable legislators to wiggle and waffle their way out of being held accountable for decisions to go to war. I had not anticipated finding the degree to which the decision to use armed force would be politicized. I had not anticipated the lengths to which presidents, presidential candidates, senators and congressmen will go to promote their own selfish political ambitions with no apparent concern for the consequences suffered by the military men and women sworn to follow the directions of these civilian leaders.

The failure of our presidents and our legislators to regard the employment of armed force as something above and removed from normal political discourse has resulted in the use of armed force that was ill advised; that was overly long in duration; and, that was overly costly in terms of blood and treasure.

I could look back on my life growing up in Westford, Massachusetts or my life in the Navy and say to myself things like: "Fool me once, shame on you. Fool me twice, shame on me;" or, "Never assume, because to assume makes an 'ass' out of 'u' and 'me'." Now that I have a son serving in the Marine Corps, I am simply angry. I am angry with a government that is poised to expand a war in Afghanistan, apparently for reasons that have more to do with the political ambitions of a president than with what is right.

The Failure of the All-Volunteer Force

After reading *AWOL: The Unexcused Absence of America's Upper Class from Military Service and How It Hurts Our Country* by Kathy

Roth-Douquet and Frank Schaeffer, I thought I would be concluding that we need to abandon the all volunteer force and revert to a selective service draft or even compulsory military service. While I think that Kathy and Frank made a compelling argument, to my surprise, I found something that I consider to be far more corrosive to the well-being of our republic – a military force shaped by political ideology.

Having grown up in Massachusetts and residing in Rhode Island for sixteen years following the conclusion of my military career, I was well aware of the New England region's attitudes toward the military. I was not prepared for the close correlation between political ideology and military recruitment that I found across the nation. A book similar to Kathy's and Frank's *AWOL* could be written that could substitute the words "Upper Class" with the words "liberals" or "Democrats."

I learned through my discussions with a very knowledgeable Army recruiting official that with few exceptions in the nation's history, the Upper Class has largely avoided military service. I also ascertained that the Army does not consider political ideology when compiling state-by-state recruiting statistics. The Army recruiters were as surprised as I was to learn of the close relationship between prevailing political ideology within individual states and voluntary military participation.

I was shocked to find that political ideology has apparently become the strongest determinant in whether or not someone volunteers for military service. Economic, religious and class distinctions appear to have less than anticipated influence on a young person's decision to serve. While Kathy and Frank bemoan the exodus of ROTC and military participation from the college campuses of elite schools like Princeton and Harvard, I believe that this exodus can better be explained by political ideology than by economic class. It is no coincidence that the elite institutions with the weakest records of military participation are located in states dominated by left-leaning political ideology.

The absence of ideological diversity that ultimately results from the present system of military participation is dangerous on many levels. From my experience in the military during the period when the effects of the draft were still being felt, I found that the discourse among officers and enlisted men with diverse political ideologies to be beneficial.

The enlisted men who served under me who were politically "lib-

160

eral" tended to challenge authority more than those men that were politically "conservative." The liberals were far more inclined to question my actions while the conservatives were more inclined to follow instructions without question. I found the frequent, at times heated, exchanges with my more liberal men to be both intellectually stimulating and thought provoking. While I seldom agreed completely with these "rabble-rousers," these exchanges <u>always</u> resulted in better decisions on my part.

Diversity of political ideology is even more critical among officers. While challenges to authority by enlisted men can impact on the operations of a single military unit, challenges to authority by officers can impact on the entire service, even the entire Department of Defense. Officers who have learned, in the words of Crosby, Stills and Nash, "to question all the answers" are far more likely to challenge the views and decisions of the civilian leadership for whom they serve. Liberal officers, or conservative officers who have been challenged by liberal men and women, are far more likely to question the decisions of their civilian leadership and far more inclined to enter into respectful debate. Officers steeped in a tradition of strong and healthy debate are far more likely to give good advice; far more likely to challenge; far more likely to resign in protest; and far less likely to blindly obey orders they know to be wrong. We need more Billy Mitchells.

As we prepare to expand our involvement in Afghanistan, where are the questions? Where is the brave officer willing to stand up and say: "We cannot fight a limited war in this place!" "We cannot justify expending a drop of blood or a penny of treasure for this cause!" "I will not lead my men in a needless war in order to validate a statement by the president that claims this to be a 'war of necessity'!" Instead, we hear carefully worded statements that express concerns; about loss of public support; about "deteriorating" conditions on the ground; about perhaps needing more troops; about perhaps needing ten more years to achieve our goals.

The current trend of military participation based on political ideology is castrating the military and along with it our ability to make wise decisions relative to fighting and winning wars. We must reverse this trend before our military leaders are completely transformed into a corps of obedient eunuchs.

Affirmative Action
and Diversity

It was not my intent to write a book about the impact of women in the military. Besides, I don't think I could have improved upon what had already been said by Stephanie Gutmann in her 2001 book entitled: *A Kinder, Gentler Military: How Political Correctness Affects Our Ability to Win Wars.* I simply touch on the subject based on my personal experience and personal observations. Having experienced a Navy in which women were largely relegated to support and administrative roles and then participated in the aggressive integration of women into most operational roles, I have learned that women have added nothing in terms of readiness for war while adding greatly as a distraction to readiness in what has been historically, what is currently, and what will always be, a male dominated profession.

My purpose in touching on affirmative action is to illustrate how pursuing a policy of anything other than a performance based criteria for military service is injurious to our ability to fight and win wars. Affirmative action based on race has a particularly insidious affect on the military at the individual, organizational and service wide levels. While I was working on this book an incident related to affirmative action came up that I thought might help to either illustrate the points I wanted to make, or, illustrate how a thoughtful affirmative action program can be administered. The incident ended up surprising me, and, disappointing me.

An element of Affirmative Action that struck close to home had to do with the subordinating of mission readiness to political correctness at my alma mater, the Naval Academy in Annapolis. Preparing to fight and win wars is now, officially, less important than having a proportionate number of Black officers serving in a profession or branch of service that they might not otherwise choose.

My suspicion is that this is not so much the result of altruism on the part of the Chief of Naval Operations and the Superintendent of the Naval Academy but rather the result of congressional "social engineering" inflicted on the military. There are possibly two phenomena at work. The first is activist Members of Congress, past and present, who have demanded that the military conform to unreasonable practices in exchange for continued congressional support for programs and systems deemed important by military leaders. The second phenomenon is the evolution of military leadership over the last decades since the end of the Viet Nam War. In the aftermath of Viet Nam and the period leading up to the First Gulf War, the formative years for today's military leadership, a higher priority was placed on military officers being good bureaucrats rather than good war fighters. Officers of this generation were encouraged (required) to seek "Washington duty" in order to further their careers. This requirement was brought about by the necessity for officers who wished to attain flag rank (all of them) to understand and to have facility with the congressional appropriations process. Show me the money!

Many of the military-hating post-Viet Nam generation of law makers sought to impose their individual wills on the armed services. Men and women members, frustrated in their attempts to impose their personal philosophies on the country as a whole, have had fewer obstacles to imposing these same philosophies onto the armed forces through the appropriations process and through the Article I Section 8 powers. Affirmative action is an example of a program, deeply rooted in society that is even more entrenched in the armed forces, even though it is contrary to the best interests of national defense.

It is not clear whether or not our military leadership actually believe that "diversity" serves our national interests. Officers are taught from an early age to not betray where unpopular orders originate. Rather, officers are taught to accept orders from higher authority as if it were their own. I prefer to believe this is the case with our current military leadership and that we have not "crossed the Rubicon" to the point where our senior military officers actually believe they are doing the right thing. That they actually believe "diversity" is more important than our ability to fight and win wars.

Unfortunately, regardless of how we got here, the end result is the same. The military, not just the Naval Academy, has embarked on a misguided course of turning our military into just another congressionally mandated "jobs program." It is now more important to artificially impose quotas on the military rather than ensuring the best possible fighting force. 3

Another disturbing aspect of the push for diversity is the impact that programs of this type have on our system of secondary and higher education. One of the questions I did get answers to from the Naval Academy was in answer to a question I had about SAT scores. While standardized test scores are used almost universally as a measurement of comparison and of selectivity among colleges and universities, I was handed a convoluted, rationalized, explanation about why the Naval Academy does not require students at the Naval Academy Prep School to take the SAT.

It is popular among the proponents of "diversity" to invalidate the SAT by claiming it to be a racially biased test mechanism not worthy of consideration. The SAT is dismissed as one of many measurements that are considered when assessing college applicants. This attitude is another way of saying: "Since I don't like what you're telling me, I refuse to believe you." This attitude would be foolish anywhere from an auto repair shop to a doctor's office, but for some reason we accept it when it comes to the SAT. The Naval Academy is simply one of many colleges and universities that has bought into this politically correct excuse.

Over the years I have listened to many people ask what is the use of having national service academies such as West Point and Annapolis? Wouldn't it be cheaper for us to send all our future officers through ROTC? The answer I have heard from our civilian and military leaders is that the national service academies are among the few ways that the federal government can demonstrate standards of excellence in education that other organizations should emulate and follow. This goal becomes an empty promise when compromises and exceptions are made in order to achieve a desired outcome. Federally sanctioned diversity programs, such as that at the Naval Academy, have an insidious affect not only on the quality of education at the Academy, but also on all of the secondary programs that produce potential applicants for admission to this and other colleges and universities. "Fudging" the numbers to achieve a desired outcome has a ripple effect downward through the entire secondary education system in our country. To borrow from Professor Flemings statement about dumbing down, well-intentioned diversity programs in colleges and universities dumb down our secondary schools as well. In the case of the Naval Academy example, we are not only dumbing down the Academy and the officer corps of the Navy, we are also contributing to the further erosion of quality in our high schools. It amounts to a deception and disgrace of national proportions in which virtually every college and university is participating. The consequences are the exact opposite of the stated intentions of the policy.

The deceit is made more egregious by underlying facts regarding SAT performance of college bound blacks nationally. Within the black population, which as previously stated is roughly 13 percent, a smaller proportion completes secondary education than the national average. In other words there is a higher drop-out rate among blacks as well as a lower percentage of black high school graduates that aspire to higher education. Of the already disproportionately low percentage of black high school graduates that are college bound, performance on the SAT Reasoning Test is significantly lower than average performance for college bound Whites. Black performance is also significantly below that of the Asian/Pacific Islander cohort as well as lagging slightly behind Hispanics and Native Americans.

The following table gives the average SAT Critical Reading and Math scores for the last twelve years. The scores are taken from data available through the Digest of Education Statistics compiled under the auspices of the U.S. Department of Education.

College Bound Seniors SAT Reasoning Test Averages

Racial/Ethnic Cohort	Critical Reading	Math
White	526.9	529.6
Hispanic	455	458
Black	431.4	425
Asian/Pacific Islander	502	568
Native American	480	482

In recent years, American colleges and universities have taken up the cause of racial and ethnic diversity. There is considerable competition among colleges and universities for the relatively few fully qualified racial and ethnic minority college bound seniors. In the drive to increase diversity, academic mediocrity has not only been condoned, it has been rewarded. Why would a college-bound African American or Hispanic student strive to excel academically in high school when the best colleges and universities accept them as they are? By accepting mediocre performance, colleges and universities are helping to perpetuate the national disgrace of a failed secondary education system, particularly for Black high school students. American colleges and universities have sent Black high school students the message that they need not apply themselves academically. Many of these same colleges and universities also send a message that athletic prowess, especially in the "big money" sports like football, is more important than academics in obtaining college admission. As the racial/ethnic mix, typical in major professional sports teams cited earlier indicates, college becomes seen as the "means" to an "end," especially for Black male high school athletes.

For a school like Harvard, which can effectively "buy" the best African American college bound seniors, the rewards to both college and student are great. Harvard gets to tout its diversity and the students get to benefit from the "Harvard brand" they graduate with. Harvard professors and administrators get to feel good about themselves for talking like "liberals" but living like "conservatives." A Harvard undergraduate degree provides the key that will open doors to the best businesses and the best post-graduate programs. In turn, these businesses and graduate programs get to tout their own diversity and the "vital" role that they play in promoting affirmative action.

For Harvard there are few if any negative consequences to this practice of rewarding mediocrity. For service academies such as the Naval Academy the consequences are potentially deadly. The service academies prepare young men and women to be leaders on the fields of battle, not in businesses and law firms. While mediocre minority businessmen and lawyers can provide "window dressing" for their respective firms, there is no such "window dressing" on the battlefield. Mediocrity on the battlefield can result in deaths.

Of course the pressure to promote diversity for the sake of diversity is not restricted to the Naval Academy. Most recently, Congress is for the first time meddling with entrance requirements at the Coast Guard Academy. Heretofore, the Coast Guard Academy has based entrance purely on merit. The Coast Guard Academy's 25 fully qualified Black cadets are apparently not enough to suite Congress. Now, Congress will mandate that the Coast Guard Academy, at one quarter the size of the other service academies, will be required to take more mediocre, less motivated, candidates than it otherwise would - more social engineering at the hands of Congress.

Afghanistan

In the main body of this book I spent a disproportionate amount of time talking about Afghanistan. Afghanistan concerns me a lot; not just because I recently attended the funeral of the young Marine Corps officer son of a Naval Academy classmate killed in Afghanistan; not just because it will be where my own young Marine Corps officer son will find himself after having already served two tours of duty in Iraq; and, not just because Afghanistan so miserably fails the "Corbett Test."

I fear that we are expanding our efforts in Afghanistan because of the pure political vanity of our president and his political party. President Obama has repeatedly referred to the War in Iraq as a "war of choice," while in the same breath, referring to the War in Afghanistan as a "war of necessity." Supposedly, a war we cannot afford to lose.

The roots of these statements can be traced back to the presidential campaign of 2004, when the Democratic candidate for president, Senator John Kerry, claimed Afghanistan to be the "the right war" as a way of criticizing President Bush, his Republican opponent, for his policies in Iraq, presumably the "bad war," the war Senator Kerry approved of but would have fought "differently." The comparison of the two wars, one being good the other being evil, allowed Senator Kerry to criticize his opponent while attempting to avoid being branded as an "anti-war liberal," a label he has been tagged with since his Viet Nam protest days.

In an article published December 9th 2008, in THE WEEK, entitled: *Will Afghanistan be Obama's Iraq?*, longtime Democratic presidential candidate advisor and political strategist/consultant, Robert Shrum confirmed this 2004 campaign strategy and how it has survived to be translated into policy by the Obama Administration. Shrum states that:

"I was part of the 2004 Kerry campaign, which elevated the idea of Afghanistan as "the right war" to conventional Democratic wisdom. This was accurate as criticism of the Bush Administration, but it was also reflexive and perhaps by now even misleading as policy. Today, we need a hard-headed examination of what's still possible, especially in light of the India-Pakistan confrontation, which could throw the entire subcontinent into further turmoil."

My fear, and what appears to be happening, is that President Obama has bought into this "conventional Democratic wisdom," and is prepared to pursue this "war of necessity" out of a misplaced desire to fulfill a campaign promise.

I have made my main points regarding Afghanistan. No matter how sympathetic we may be to the plight of Afghanistan; no matter how much we would like to track down and "bring to justice" the perpetrators of the 9/11 attacks; we are no more able to solve the Afghanistan dilemma than Britain and the Soviet Union were in centuries past. What makes us think we can succeed where the Soviet Union, using a virtually unlimited, "scorched earth," strategy, failed in attaining essentially the same objective?

Though not directly related to the main premise of this book, while doing background research two issues related to Afghanistan surprised me – (1) the terms of the Durand Treaty, and (2) the genesis of Afghanistan's role in world heroin trade. I have come to the opinion that a lasting solution to the enigma of Afghanistan may reside in these two issues rather than in a military solution.

Durand Treaty of 1893 and Its Lasting Impact

I remember reading a book as part of my college major in Far Easter Studies/Mandarin Chinese. The book was *Foreign Mud: Being an Account of the Opium Imbroglio at Canton in the 1830s and the Anglo-Chinese War That Followed* by Maurice Collis and first published in 1946. *Foreign Mud* explains how Britain, under the guise of open trade with China, pushed opium, cultivated on British plantations in India, upon China. When China resisted this "trade," Britain went to war in order to assure an open market for its goods. Two wars were fought between Britain and China over opium. China lost both wars. Not only did China lose militarily but also China was "required" to continue its involuntary "addiction" to opiates.

As part of the settlement of the first of these "opium wars," Britain acquired Hong Kong as a colony and as a port of entry for its "products" through the Treaty of Nanking of 1842. This treaty was subsequently renegotiated in the 1890s, giving Britain a 99 year lease on the island.

This same sort of arrangement was struck between Britain and Afghanistan in the 1890s. The Durand Treaty of 1893 stripped Afghanistan of roughly half of its territory as well as its connection to the sea.

During the 1990s, Britain and China entered into negotiations to fulfill Britain's obligations under its 99-year lease of Hong Kong. A peaceful transfer of Hong Kong to China was carried out in 1997. Afghanistan looked on in envy, and resentment, as no similar negotiations took place to fulfill the similar obligations under the Durand Treaty which conveyed to Pakistan. Afghanistan remains landlocked and ethnic Afghans remain separated from their homeland.

It seems to me that the United States could help to remove a major obstacle to regional peace by brokering a negotiated resolution to the unfulfilled promise of the Durand Treaty. While the return of its territory may not resolve Afghanistan's internal political problems it would be the right thing to do and it might provide a necessary first step in resolving long simmering regional issues.

Heroin and the War on Drugs

The large scale commercial production of opium by Britain in the early 1800s essentially let the "genie out of the bottle." Britain's mass cultivation of poppies for the purpose of extracting opium, vastly expanded upon an ancient practice or using opiates to relieve pain. Opium also had a widespread following among recreational users seeking to experience euphoria. The opium cultivation along with the opium trade and the opium wars with China opened the door to the worldwide use of opiates.

Despite efforts to regulate and prohibit the use of opiates, beginning in the early 20th Century, demand for non-medicinal (recreational) use of opiates has essentially remained constant. "Controlled" use and production of opium derivatives has grown. Beginning with its first commercially manufactured derivative, heroin, and continuing with the currently popular prescribed pain reliever oxycodone, (also known by its time-release form of OxyContin®), scientists have repeatedly attempted to create a pain reliever without adverse side effects and addictive properties. So far, these efforts have failed. Abuse of, and addiction to legally manufactured, transported and sold opiates, has only expanded the universe of recreational use and abuse of opiates.

The fact that Afghanistan currently leads the world in producing the illegal opium derivative, heroin, did not really surprise me. What did surprise me was the comparison of the pain relieving/euphoria inducing heroin production in the late 19th Century with the production of the common household stimulants – tea and coffee. In 1890, heroin availability rivaled that of tea and coffee. That got my attention.

During my early days as a shipboard naval officer, I was a regular "coffee abuser." I learned to drink coffee strong and black as a matter of necessity rather than of choice. Long work hours and long night watches on the ship's bridge led to a dependency on caffeine. Coffee became the "drug of choice" aboard all ships of the United States Navy when alcohol was totally banned by Secretary of the Navy, Josephus Daniels in 1914. I learned of the "addictive qualities" of caffeine shortly after reporting to shore duty for the first time. When I kept up with my shipboard coffee habits, I found myself having chest pressure and shaky hands. Suspecting caffeine to be the culprit, I cut out coffee drinking – "cold turkey." I suffered through roughly three weeks of headaches, daytime drowsiness, and general irritability before being freed of coffee's grip. I still like coffee, strong and black – just decaf though.

Years later, while qualifying to become a coffee roaster, I learned that coffee is second in value to petroleum as a commodity on the world market. Coffee growing is somewhat restricted as to where it can be successfully grown. Nevertheless, coffee is commercially grown in diverse places around the world. My favorite varieties come from places such as coffee's ancestral home, Ethiopia; the island of Sumatra; Columbia; and, Kona in the Hawaiian island chain.

While not as important on the world market as coffee, tea remains hugely popular worldwide as a source of the stimulant drug - caffeine. I bring this up in order to pose the question: What would be the reaction of the world market if coffee and tea were to be banned in the same way that opiates were banned?

We can probably get a "window" into how difficult it would be to ban coffee or tea by recalling alcohol prohibition – as with alcohol it would most likely lead to widespread unlawful distribution and ultimate failure in regulating consumption. We might even see a mass uprising of the legions of men and women who daily get their caffeine fixes from "caffeine dens" like Starbucks and Dunkin Donuts.

For many who consume opiates for non-medicinal/recreational purposes, there is little difference between the use of opium derivatives and the use of alcohol, caffeine, and their close cousin, nicotine. The same thing can be said for users of other widely used illegal substances such as cocaine and marijuana.

The production and consumption of opiates, since being regulated early in the 20th Century, has been predictable. Like with alcohol during the prohibition period between 1920 and 1933, illegal production and consumption continues. Unlike the alcohol prohibition period, the production, transport and consumption of opiates has had a much longer duration to expand. Today, the production, transport and consumption of opiates and other controlled substances constitutes a vast "underground" economy that undermines the economies and cultures of many countries, Afghanistan among them.

The heroin trade is a double-edged sword when it comes to the threat that it poses to countries, such as the United States, that wish to stop or at least hinder this trade. The detrimental effects of heroin addiction on users is well documented; however, perhaps even worse is the impact that heroin trade has on non-users who are victim to the various tentacles of the trade itself. Revenue from heroin production, while not taxed by organized nation-states is nevertheless taxed by a criminal and terrorist underground. Heroin revenue is the principal source of income for the force we are supposedly at war with – Al Qaeda. It is heroin revenue that pays for the mountain training camps; buys the materials for the Improvised Explosive Devises (IEDs); pays compensation to the families of suicide bombers; and, pays bribes to government and law enforcement officials. We, in the United States, often hear the phrase: "money is the mother's milk of politics." In this case it is heroin that is the "mother's milk" of international terrorism.

Of course, the cultivation of poppies and other plants to support the underground narcotics market is not isolated to the mountain valleys of Afghanistan. Of perhaps even greater concern to narcotics consuming nations, such as the United States, is the proliferation of heroin production to countries such as Mexico. Mexico, long a country of dubious legal standards and ethics in government, is at risk of falling under the control of drug cartels. A state of civil war exists in Mexico as the national government attempts to take back control of vast areas of the country from the cartels. The Mexican Army has been called into the battle because the cartels have either killed or co-opted large numbers of local and regional law enforcement officials. Perhaps more alarmingly, Mexican drug cartels have set up "offices" in virtually every corner of the United States from which the shipment and delivery of illegal narcotics is managed. Like the Taliban and Al Qaeda in Afghanistan, "street gangs" throughout the United States are increasingly being armed and financed by Mexican drug cartel revenues. It is the ultimate irony that drug revenues generated in the wealthy user nations are financing the violent undermining and potential demise of these very same user nations, the United States being among them.

So far, the response to this threat has been a nearly four decades long "War on Drugs" that includes military action against heroin production in Afghanistan. Recent action in Afghanistan has changed from a strictly poppy eradication strategy to a strategy that includes undermining actual heroin production and shipment. In another ironic twist, the effort to eradicate opium production in Afghanistan may serve to eliminate that country's principal cash crop and at the same time undermine the very government we have worked so hard to foster. The eradication of poppies and heroin from Afghanistan is anything but a "win-win" proposition.

In addition to the costly and probably futile efforts in Afghanistan, the United States and its western allies continue to wage an even more costly and demonstrably futile effort in the international war on the production, shipment and sale of illegal drugs. In the United States, this effort is being fought at the three levels of production, shipment and sale. To a far lesser extent, the war is being fought at the end-user level.

A quick look at the commitment to eradicating illegal drugs in terms of people and infrastructure shows for example that the United States Drug Enforcement Administration (DEA) has 227 domestic offices in the fifty states and Puerto Rico. It has 87 foreign offices located in 63 different countries. The DEA is the lead agency for drug eradication but by no means the only agency involved. At least twelve other major agencies and departments, including the Defense Department, play major roles in the overall war effort. In figures compiled by the non-profit organization, Drug Sense, the monetary as well as human costs are summarized. According to statistics drawn from the Office of National Drug Policy (ONDCP), the annual federal budgetary cost now exceeds $20 billion. The combined cost to local and state governments exceeds $30 billion. And, according to FBI and Department of Justice statistics, roughly 1.8 million people are incarcerated annually for drug offenses, a number that constitutes approximately 25 percent of all people incarcerated in the United States.

The mere suggestion of liberalizing or lifting prohibition laws is, like suggesting changes to Social Security, a "third rail" to politics – touch it and you die. The result has been a continued costly and futile war on drugs, more doing the same thing over and over and expecting different results. The prospect of repealing prohibition of drugs, similar to what was done in 1933 with the repeal of the prohibition of alcohol, is worthy of consideration. In a December 2008 scholarly article, entitled *The Budgetary Implications of Drug Prohibition* by Jeffrey A. Miron of the Department of Economics at Harvard University, Mr. Miron reports that legalization of drugs would result in approximately $44.1 billion in annual savings and potentially $32.7 billion in tax revenue. When coupled with the potential savings in both monetary and human terms related arrests and incarcerations, the potential annual net gain exceeds $100 billion.

Perhaps most beneficial for countries such as Afghanistan is the long term potential gain of bringing the huge international market for currently prohibited substances out of the shadows and into the light of day. By instituting national and international regulation and control of the cultivation, processing, shipment and sale of substances like heroin, a major step could be taken toward shutting down the invasive and sinister effects of the underworld narco-economy. The laws of supply and demand as applied to narcotics could be controlled in much the same way as for other widely used commodities such as coffee and tea. The change in approach to control of narcotics would also place the onus for confronting narcotics' ever-present evil side on the "users" rather than the "producers." A change in approach would once and for all recognize that it is the "user states" like Britain that created the mess in the first place and it is the "user states," especially the United States, that sustain it. A change of approach may not be able to put the "genie back in the bottle" but it would at least force the genie to serve its rightful master.

A model for a new approach to narcotics can best be found in the alcohol prohibition experience of the last century. While the repeal of prohibition with the enactment of the 21st Amendment to the Constitution failed to remove the ever-present evil side of alcohol, it did succeed in largely eradicating the criminal production, transport and sale of the substance; it did decriminalize the use of alcohol by its consumers; it did succeed in reducing the costs related to law enforcement; and, it did succeed in creating a new "sin tax" revenue source.

We have all heard the famous quote (and its variants) from George Santayana – "Those who cannot remember the past are doomed to repeat it." With regard to Afghanistan, we are demonstrating that we are not only capable, but also inclined toward repeating the errors of the past. The United States and its NATO allies are marching down the very same roads that Britain and the Soviet Union marched down before us.

For the purpose of confronting the dilemma of narcotics; a situation in which there is no ideal solution; yet a situation that is at the core of the Afghanistan conundrum, I prefer to refer to another philosopher. In attempting to convince the warring city states of 16th Century Italy to learn from the lessons of the Roman republic, Machiavelli, in the introductory comments to his *Discourses on Livy,* urged leaders to appreciate history, not just for its people, places, things and chronology, but for the practices and policies that can be imitated. In confronting the dilemma of narcotics, there is much to be learned, and imitated, from the successful practices and policies of the past.

Command of the Seas

The final point that I am going to make does not fit into the "surprise" category. It is more something that I perhaps had taken for granted

175

or never fully appreciated. In reading through Julian Corbett's *Some Principles of Maritime Strategy,* I was reawakened to the absolutely important role "command of the seas" plays in our existence as a free nation. Though covered in a tangential manner as but one of the criteria to be met in order to pursue limited war, command of the seas is a matter that deserves special note.

To reiterate, command of the seas is a necessary element of our defense strategy to assure the survival of the homeland while also being able to deny the command of the territorial seas adjacent to a remote and limited territorial object. We have been repeatedly reminded throughout our history of the impact that command of the seas plays in assuring seaborne commerce. Seizure of commercial shipping off the Somali coast by pirates has provided us with the most recent reminder.

There are, however, sides to command of the seas that were not mentioned or envisioned by Julian Corbett. Command of the seas can be threatened by the times and command of the seas can in turn threaten the times.

At the present time, there are a number of circumstances that could lead to the United States "letting its guard down" relative to command of the seas. One circumstance is that the United States is virtually unchallenged by any other naval power. As in other periods in history, there are strong urges to forgo the high expense of maintaining a strong peacetime navy. It is very tempting for Congress to cut defense spending in order to pursue domestic priorities. One example of succumbing to this temptation has been carried on as part of the post Cold War "peace dividend." If there is any lesson to be learned from the two world wars and the Cold War, it is the importance of the submarine to taking and retaining command of the seas. Yet, in recent years the submarine force has been cut drastically with little or no public notice. Our ability to reverse the decline in both submarines and submariners is quickly vanishing.

A second condition of the times is the current war in Iraq and Afghanistan. Both wars have been land wars with the fighting done primarily by forces of the Army and Marine Corps. Navy and Air Force involvement in these wars has largely been considered of secondary or tertiary importance. Naval and air forces have been largely unchallenged.

In recognition of this condition, the strength of the Army and Marine Corps has been bolstered while the Navy and the Air Force have been diminished. Again, the decline in numbers of ships and aircraft and the highly trained technicians that operate them will be very difficult to reverse should a national emergency necessitate a ramped-up role for these services.

Due to the major down-turn in the national economy coincident with these wars, there is a strong inclination to look for ways to cut costs. The Defense Department, having the largest single category of discretionary spending by the national government, becomes the most logical place to cut these costs. Within the Defense Department, the Navy and the Air Force, with their expensive weapons systems, are the most "inviting" targets for these cuts. Aside from the fact that the United States is dependent on the Navy and the Air Force for the security of the homeland, the very weapons systems that make these services so expensive and so complex, take many years to design, build and field. A wholesale early retirement of some of these systems can lead to a dangerous and potentially permanent loss of military capability. When the need for replacements of these systems is recognized, it is often too late or too expensive. In recent years, there have been noteworthy examples of failed shipbuilding or aircraft building programs that have left key capabilities, critical to national security, in peril.

Closely related to this failure is the coincident loss of the ability to recover. The United States, while still a maritime, island nation, dependent on the sea, has lost much of its capacity to build ships at all. There is now only one shipyard that has the skills, facilities, and capability to build aircraft carriers. Only one company is capable of constructing submarines. There are serious problems with the quality of entire classes of surface ships being constructed. There are currently no shipyards, owned and operated by the Navy, capable of constructing warships. The almost total loss of competition in the shipbuilding industry has driven up costs to the point where fleet strength cannot be maintained. The ability to "flex" to a higher level of production in a national emergency has essentially been lost.

Perhaps most troubling is the possibility that command of the seas, directed by a civilian government almost totally void of military experience, could be used for the wrong reasons. There are ample examples of how Britain, France, Spain, Japan, and to a lesser extent, other European seafaring nations have used sea power for the wrong reasons. While the United States prides itself as being a "liberator" rather than an "occupier," it does not take too much of a stretch of imagination to see the line between liberation and occupation becoming blurred. One can foresee a time where sea power is used, not because we should, but simply because we can.

Speaking to Chairman of the Joint Chiefs, General Colin Powell, then U.N. Ambassador, Madeleine Albright said:

"What's the point of having this superb military you're always talking about if we can't use it?"

My main concern about an attitude, like that expressed by Madeleine Albright, is it will be coupled with a partisan and politicized "statutory authorization" leading to dangerous military adventurism. My fear is that an administration with this attitude toward the (mis)use of the military aided and abetted by a compliant Congress, will lead to repeated entry into armed conflicts not because we should but simply because we can; repeated cases of doing the same thing over and over and expecting different results – INSANITY!

Appendices

Appendix I - Article I Section 8

(Enumerated Powers of Congress)

The Congress shall have Power To lay and collect Taxes, Duties, Imposts and Excises, to pay the Debts and provide for the common Defence and general Welfare of the United States; but all Duties, Imposts and Excises shall be uniform throughout the United States;

To borrow money on the credit of the United States;

To regulate Commerce with foreign Nations, and among the several States, and with the Indian Tribes;

To establish an uniform Rule of Naturalization, and uniform Laws on the subject of Bankruptcies throughout the United States;

To coin Money, regulate the Value thereof, and of foreign Coin, and fix the Standard of Weights and Measures;

To provide for the Punishment of counterfeiting the Securities and current Coin of the United States;

To establish Post Offices and Post Roads;

To promote the Progress of Science and useful Arts, by securing for limited Times to Authors and Inventors the exclusive Right to their respective Writings and Discoveries;

To constitute Tribunals inferior to the supreme Court;

To define and punish Piracies and Felonies committed on the high Seas, and Offenses against the Law of Nations;

To declare War, grant Letters of Marque and Reprisal, and make Rules concerning Captures on Land and Water;

To raise and support Armies, but no Appropriation of Money to that Use shall be for a longer Term than two Years;

To provide and maintain a Navy;

To make Rules for the Government and Regulation of the land and naval Forces;

To provide for calling forth the Militia to execute the Laws of the Union, suppress Insurrections and repel Invasions;

To provide for organizing, arming, and disciplining the Militia, and for governing such Part of them as may be employed in the Service of the United States, reserving to the States respectively, the Appointment of the Officers, and the Authority of training the Militia according to the discipline prescribed by Congress;

To exercise exclusive Legislation in all Cases whatsoever, over such District (not exceeding ten Miles square) as may, by Cession of particular States, and the acceptance of Congress, become the Seat of the Government of the United States, and to exercise like Authority over all Places purchased by the Consent of the Legislature of the State in which the Same shall be, for the Erection of Forts, Magazines, Arsenals, dock-Yards, and other needful Buildings; And

To make all Laws which shall be necessary and proper for carrying into Execution the foregoing Powers, and all other Powers vested by this Constitution in the Government of the United States, or in any Department or Officer thereof.

Appendix II - Tonkin Gulf Resolution

"To promote the maintenance of international peace and security in Southeast Asia.

"Whereas naval units of the communist regime in Vietnam, in violation of the principles of the Charter of the United Nations and of international law, have deliberately and repeatedly attacked United States naval vessels lawfully present in international waters, and have thereby created a serious threat to international peace; and

"Whereas these attacks are part of a deliberate and systematic campaign of aggression that the communist regime in North Vietnam has been waging against its neighbors and the nations joined with them in the collective defense of their freedom; and

"Whereas the United States is assisting the peoples of Southeast Asia to protect their freedom and has no territorial, military or political ambitions in that area, but desires only that these peoples should be left in peace to work out their own destinies in their own way: Now, therefore, be it

"*Resolved by the Senate and House of Representatives of the United States of America in Congress assembled,* That the Congress approves and supports the determination of the President, as Commander in Chief, to take all necessary measures to repel any armed attack against the forces of the United States and to prevent further aggression.

"Sec. 2. The United States regards as vital to its national interest and to world peace the maintenance of international peace and security in Southeast Asia. Consonant with the Constitution of the United States and the Charter of the United Nations and in accordance with its obligations under the Southeast Asia Collective Defense Treaty, the United States is, therefore, prepared, as

181

the President determines, to take all necessary steps, including the use of armed force, to assist any member or protocol state of the Southeast Asia Collective Defense Treaty requesting assistance in defense of its freedom.

"Sec. 3. This resolution shall expire when the President shall determine that the peace and security of the area is reasonably assured by international conditions created by action of the United Nations or otherwise, except that it may be terminated earlier by concurrent resolution of the Congress."

Appendix III - War Powers Resolution (P.L. 93-148)

Public Law 93-148
93rd Congress, H. J. Res. 542
November 7, 1973

Joint Resolution

Concerning the War Powers of Congress and the President.

Resolved by the Senate and the House of Representatives of the United States of America in Congress assembled,

SHORT TITLE

SECTION 1. This joint resolution may be cited as the "War Powers Resolution".

PURPOSE AND POLICY

SEC. 2. (a) It is the purpose of this joint resolution to fulfill the intent of the framers of the Constitution of the United States and insure that the collective judgement of both the Congress and the President will apply to the introduction of United States Armed Forces into hostilities, or into situations where imminent involvement in hostilities is clearly indicated by the circumstances, and to the continued use of such forces in hostilities or in such situations.

(b) Under article I, section 8, of the Constitution, it is specifically provided that the Congress shall have the power to make all laws necessary and proper for carrying into execution, not only its own powers but also all other powers vested by the Constitution in the Government of the United States, or in any department or officer thereof.

(c) The constitutional powers of the President as Commander-in-Chief to introduce United States Armed Forces into hostilities, or into situations where imminent involvement in hostilities is clearly indicated by the circumstances, are exercised only pursuant to (1) a declaration of war, (2) specific statutory authorization, or (3) a national emergency created by attack upon the United States, its territories or possessions, or its armed forces.

CONSULTATION

SEC. 3. The President in every possible instance shall consult with Congress before introducing United States Armed Forces into hostilities or into situation where imminent involvement in hostilities is clearly indicated by the circumstances, and after every such introduction shall consult regularly with the Congress until United States Armed Forces are no longer engaged in hostilities or have been removed from such situations.

REPORTING

SEC. 4. (a) In the absence of a declaration of war, in any case in which United States Armed Forces are introduced—

(1) into hostilities or into situations where imminent involvement in hostilities is clearly indicated by the circumstances;

(2) into the territory, airspace or waters of a foreign nation, while equipped for combat, except for deployments which relate solely to supply, replacement, repair, or training of such forces; or

(3) in numbers which substantially enlarge United States Armed Forces equipped for combat already located in a foreign nation; the president shall submit within 48 hours to the Speaker of the House of Representatives and to the President pro tempore of the Senate a report, in writing, setting forth—

(A) the circumstances necessitating the introduction of United States Armed Forces;

(B) the constitutional and legislative authority under which such introduction took place; and

(C) the estimated scope and duration of the hostilities or involvement.

(b) The President shall provide such other information as the Congress may request in the fulfillment of its constitutional responsibilities with respect to committing the Nation to war and to the use of United States Armed Forces abroad

(c) Whenever United States Armed Forces are introduced into hostilities or into any situation described in subsection (a) of this section, the President shall, so long as such armed forces continue to be engaged in such hostilities or situation, report to the Congress periodically on the status of such hostilities or situation as well as on the scope and duration of such hostilities or situation, but in no event shall he report to the Congress less often than once every six months.

CONGRESSIONAL ACTION

SEC. 5. (a) Each report submitted pursuant to section 4(a)(1) shall be transmitted to the Speaker of the House of Representatives and to the President pro tempore of the Senate on the same calendar day. Each report so transmitted shall be referred to the Committee on Foreign Affairs of the House of Representatives and to the Committee on Foreign Relations of the Senate for appropriate action. If, when the report is transmitted, the Congress has adjourned sine die or has adjourned for any period in excess of three calendar days, the Speaker of the House of Representatives and the President pro tempore of the Senate, if they deem it advisable (or if petitioned by at least 30 percent of the membership of their respective Houses) shall jointly request the President to convene Congress in order that it may consider the report and take appropriate action pursuant to this section.

(b) Within sixty calendar days after a report is submitted or is required to be submitted pursuant to section 4(a)(1), whichever is earlier, the President shall terminate any use of United States Armed Forces with respect to which such report was submitted (or required to be submitted), unless the Congress (1) has declared war or has enacted a specific authorization for such use of United States Armed Forces, (2) has extended by law such sixty-day period, or (3) is physically unable to meet as a result of an armed attack upon the United States. Such sixty-day period shall be extended for not more than an additional thirty days if the President determines and certifies to the Congress in writing that unavoidable military necessity respecting the safety of United States Armed Forces requires the continued use of such armed forces in the course of bringing about a prompt removal of such forces.

(c) Notwithstanding subsection (b), at any time that United States Armed Forces are engaged in hostilities outside the territory of the United States, its possessions and territories without a declaration of war or specific statutory authorization, such forces shall be removed by the President if the Congress so directs by concurrent resolution.

CONGRESSIONAL PRIORITY PROCEDURES FOR JOINT RESOLUTION OR BILL

SEC. 6. (a) Any joint resolution or bill introduced pursuant to section 5(b) at least thirty calendar days before the expiration of the sixty-day period specified in such section shall be referred to the Committee on Foreign Affairs of the House of Representatives or the Committee on Foreign Relations of the Senate, as the case may be, and such committee shall report one such joint resolution or bill, together with its recommendations, not later than twenty-four calendar days before the expiration of the sixty-day period specified in such section, unless such House shall otherwise determine by the yeas and nays.

(b) Any joint resolution or bill so reported shall become the pending business of the House in question (in the case of the Senate the time for debate shall be equally divided between the proponents and the opponents), and shall be voted on within three calendar days thereafter, unless such House shall otherwise determine by yeas and nays.

(c) Such a joint resolution or bill passed by one House shall be referred to the committee of the other House named in subsection (a) and shall be reported out not later than fourteen calendar days before the expiration

186

of the sixty-day period specified in section 5(b). The joint resolution or bill so reported shall become the pending business of the House in question and shall be voted on within three calendar days after it has been reported, unless such House shall otherwise determine by yeas and nays.

(d) In the case of any disagreement between the two Houses of Congress with respect to a joint resolution or bill passed by both Houses, conferees shall be promptly appointed and the committee of conference shall make and file a report with respect to such resolution or bill not later than four calendar days before the expiration of the sixty-day period specified in section 5(b). In the event the conferees are unable to agree within 48 hours, they shall report back to their respective Houses in disagreement. Notwithstanding any rule in either House concerning the printing of conference reports in the Record or concerning any delay in the consideration of such reports, such report shall be acted on by both Houses not later than the expiration of such sixty-day period.

CONGRESSIONAL PRIORITY PROCEDURES FOR CONCURRENT RESOLUTION

SEC. 7. (a) Any concurrent resolution introduced pursuant to section 5(b) at least thirty calendar days before the expiration of the sixty-day period specified in such section shall be referred to the Committee on Foreign Affairs of the House of Representatives or the Committee on Foreign Relations of the Senate, as the case may be, and one such concurrent resolution shall be reported out by such committee together with its recommendations within fifteen calendar days, unless such House shall otherwise determine by the yeas and nays.

(b) Any concurrent resolution so reported shall become the pending business of the House in question (in the case of the Senate the time for debate shall be equally divided between the proponents and the opponents), and shall be voted on within three calendar days thereafter, unless such House shall otherwise determine by yeas and nays.

(c) Such a concurrent resolution passed by one House shall be referred to the committee of the other House named in subsection (a) and shall be reported out by such committee together with its recommendations within fifteen calendar days and shall thereupon become the pending business of such House and shall be voted on within three calendar days after it has been reported, unless such House shall otherwise determine by yeas and nays.

(d) In the case of any disagreement between the two Houses of Congress with respect to a concurrent resolution passed by both Houses, conferees shall be promptly appointed and the committee of conference shall make and file a report with respect to such concurrent resolution within six calendar days after the legislation is referred to the committee of conference. Notwithstanding any rule in either House concerning the printing of conference reports in the Record or concerning any delay in the consideration of such reports, such report shall be acted on by both Houses not later than six calendar days after the conference report is filed. In the event the conferees are unable to agree within 48 hours, they shall report back to their respective Houses in disagreement.

INTERPRETATION OF JOINT RESOLUTION

SEC. 8. (a) Authority to introduce United States Armed Forces into hostilities or into situations wherein involvement in hostilities is clearly indicated by the circumstances shall not be inferred—

(1) from any provision of law (whether or not in effect before the date of the enactment of this joint resolution), including any provision contained in any appropriation Act, unless such provision specifically authorizes the introduction of United States Armed Forces into hostilities or into such situations and stating that it is intended to constitute specific statutory authorization within the meaning of this joint resolution; or

(2) from any treaty heretofore or hereafter ratified unless such treaty is implemented by legislation specifically authorizing the introduction of United States Armed Forces into hostilities or into such situations and stating that it is intended to constitute specific statutory authorization within the meaning of this joint resolution.

(b) Nothing in this joint resolution shall be construed to require any further specific statutory authorization to permit members of United States

Armed Forces to participate jointly with members of the armed forces of one or more foreign countries in the headquarters operations of high-level military commands which were established prior to the date of enactment of this joint resolution and pursuant to the United Nations Charter or any treaty ratified by the United States prior to such date.

(c) For purposes of this joint resolution, the term "introduction of United States Armed Forces" includes the assignment of member of such armed forces to command, coordinate, participate in the movement of, or accompany the regular or irregular military forces of any foreign country or government when such military forces are engaged, or there exists an imminent threat that such forces will become engaged, in hostilities.

(d) Nothing in this joint resolution—

> (1) is intended to alter the constitutional authority of the Congress or of the President, or the provision of existing treaties; or

> (2) shall be construed as granting any authority to the President with respect to the introduction of United States Armed Forces into hostilities or into situations wherein involvement in hostilities is clearly indicated by the circumstances which authority he would not have had in the absence of this joint resolution.

SEPARABILITY CLAUSE

SEC. 9. If any provision of this joint resolution or the application thereof to any person or circumstance is held invalid, the remainder of the joint resolution and the application of such provision to any other person or circumstance shall not be affected thereby.

EFFECTIVE DATE

SEC. 10. This joint resolution shall take effect on the date of its enactment.

CARL ALBERT
Speaker of the House of Representatives.

JAMES O. EASTLAND
President of the Senate pro tempore.

189

IN THE HOUSE OF REPRESENTATIVES, U.S.,

November 7, 1973.

The House of Representatives having proceeded to reconsider the resolution (H. J. Res 542) entitled "Joint resolution concerning the war powers of Congress and the President", returned by the President of the United States with his objections, to the House of Representatives, in which it originated, it was

Resolved, That the said resolution pass, two-thirds of the House of Representatives agreeing to pass the same.

Attest:
W. PAT JENNINGS
Clerk.

I certify that this Joint Resolution originated in the House of Representatives.

W. PAT JENNINGS
Clerk.

IN THE SENATE OF THE UNITED STATES

November 7, 1973

The Senate having proceeded to reconsider the joint resolution (H. J. Res. 542) entitled "Joint resolution concerning the war powers of Congress and the President", returned by the President of the United States with his objections to the House of Representatives, in which it originate, it was

Resolved, That the said joint resolution pass, two-thirds of the Senators present having voted in the affirmative.

Attest:
FRANCIS R. VALEO
Secretary.

Appendix IV - Iraq Breach Resolution (P.L. 105-235)

[DOCID: f:publ235.105]

[[Page 1537]]

IRAQI BREACH OF INTERNATIONAL OBLIGATIONS

[[Page 112 STAT. 1538]]

Public Law 105-235
105th Congress
Joint Resolution

Finding the Government of Iraq in unacceptable and material breach of its international obligations. <<NOTE: Aug. 14, 1998 - [S.J. Res. 54]>>

Whereas hostilities in Operation Desert Storm ended on February 28, 1991, and the conditions governing the cease-fire were specified in United Nations Security Council Resolutions 686 (March 2, 1991) and 687 (April 3, 1991);

Whereas United Nations Security Council Resolution 687 requires that international economic sanctions remain in place until Iraq discloses and destroys its weapons of mass destruction programs and capabilities and undertakes unconditionally never to resume such activities;

Whereas Resolution 687 established the United Nations Special Commission on Iraq (UNSCOM) to uncover all aspects of Iraq's weapons of mass destruction programs and tasked the Director-General of the International Atomic Energy Agency to locate and remove or destroy all nuclear weapons systems, subsystems or material from Iraq;

191

Whereas United Nations Security Council Resolution 715, adopted on October 11, 1991, empowered UNSCOM to maintain a long-term monitoring program to ensure Iraq's weapons of mass destruction programs are dismantled and not restarted;

Whereas Iraq has consistently fought to hide the full extent of its weapons programs, and has systematically made false declarations to the Security Council and to UNSCOM regarding those programs, and has systematically obstructed weapons inspections for seven years;

Whereas in June 1991, Iraqi forces fired on International Atomic Energy Agency inspectors and otherwise obstructed and misled UNSCOM inspectors, resulting in United Nations Security Council Resolution 707 which found Iraq to be in "material breach" of its obligations under United Nations Security Council Resolution 687 for failing to allow UNSCOM inspectors access to a site storing nuclear equipment;

Whereas in January and February of 1992, Iraq rejected plans to install long-term monitoring equipment and cameras called for in United Nations resolutions, resulting in a Security Council Presidential Statement of February 19, 1992 which declared that Iraq was in "continuing material breach" of its obligations;

Whereas in February of 1992, Iraq continued to obstruct the installation of monitoring equipment, and failed to comply with UNSCOM orders to allow destruction of missiles and other proscribed weapons, resulting in the Security Council Presidential Statement of February 28, 1992, which reiterated that Iraq was in "continuing material breach" and noted a "further material

[[Page 112 STAT. 1539]]

breach" on account of Iraq's failure to allow destruction of ballistic missile equipment;

192

Whereas on July 5, 1992, Iraq denied UNSCOM inspectors access to the Iraqi Ministry of Agriculture, resulting in a Security Council Presidential Statement of July 6, 1992, which declared that Iraq was in "material and unacceptable breach" of its obligations under United Nations resolutions;

Whereas in December of 1992 and January of 1993, Iraq violated the southern no-fly zone, moved surface-to-air missiles into the no-fly zone, raided a weapons depot in internationally recognized Kuwaiti territory and denied landing rights to a plane carrying United Nations weapons inspectors, resulting in a Security Council Presidential Statement of January 8, 1993, which declared that Iraq was in an "unacceptable and material breach" of its obligations under United Nations resolutions;

Whereas in response to continued Iraqi defiance, a Security Council Presidential Statement of January 11, 1993, reaffirmed the previous finding of material breach, followed on January 13 and 18 by allied air raids, and on January 17 with an allied missile attack on Iraqi targets;

Whereas on June 10, 1993, Iraq prevented UNSCOM's installation of cameras and monitoring equipment, resulting in a Security Council Presidential Statement of June 18, 1993, declaring Iraq's refusal to comply to be a "material and unacceptable breach";

Whereas on October 6, 1994, Iraq threatened to end cooperation with weapons inspectors if sanctions were not ended, and one day later, massed 10,000 troops within 30 miles of the Kuwaiti border, resulting in United Nations Security Council Resolution 949 demanding Iraq's withdrawal from the Kuwaiti border area and renewal of compliance with UNSCOM;

Whereas on April 10, 1995, UNSCOM reported to the Security Council that Iraq had concealed its biological weapons program, and had

193

failed to account for 17 tons of biological weapons material resulting in the Security Council's renewal of sanctions against Iraq;

Whereas on July 1, 1995, Iraq admitted to a full scale biological weapons program, but denied weaponization of biological agents, and subsequently threatened to end cooperation with UNSCOM resulting in the Security Council's renewal of sanctions against Iraq;

Whereas on March 8, 11, 14, and 15, 1996, Iraq again barred UNSCOM inspectors from sites containing documents and weapons, in response to which the Security Council issued a Presidential Statement condemning "clear violations by Iraq of previous Resolutions 687, 707, and 715";

Whereas from June 11-15, 1996, Iraq repeatedly barred weapons inspectors from military sites, in response to which the Security Council adopted United Nations Security Council Resolution 1060, noting the "clear violation on United Nations Security Council Resolutions 687, 707, and 715" and in response to Iraq's continued violations, issued a Presidential Statement detailing Iraq's "gross violation of obligations";

Whereas in August 1996, Iraqi troops overran Irbil, in Iraqi Kurdistan, employing more than 30,000 troops and Republican Guards, in response to which the Security Council briefly suspended implementation on United Nations Security Council Resolution 986, the United Nations oil for food plan;

[[Page 112 STAT. 1540]]

Whereas in December 1996, Iraq prevented UNSCOM from removing 130 Scud missile engines from Iraq for analysis, resulting in a Security Council Presidential Statement which "deplore[d]" Iraq's refusal to cooperate with UNSCOM;

Whereas on April 9, 1997, Iraq violated the no-fly zone in southernIraq and United Nations Security Council Resolution 670, banning international flights, resulting in a Security Council statement regretting Iraq's lack of "specific consultation" with the Council;

194

Whereas on June 4 and 5, 1997 Iraqi officials on board UNSCOM aircraft interfered with the controls and inspections, endangering inspectors and obstructing the UNSCOM mission, resulting in a United Nations Security Council Presidential Statement demanding Iraq end its interference and on June 21, 1997, United Nations Security Council Resolution 1115 threatened sanctions on Iraqi officials responsible for these interferences;

Whereas on September 13, 1997, during an inspection mission, an Iraqi official attacked UNSCOM officials engaged in photographing illegal Iraqi activities, resulting in the October 23, 1997, adoption of United Nations Security Council Resolution 1134 which threatened a travel ban on Iraqi officials responsible for noncompliance with United Nations resolutions;

Whereas on October 29, 1997, Iraq announced that it would no longer allow American inspectors working with UNSCOM to conduct inspections in Iraq, blocking UNSCOM teams containing Americans to conduct inspections and threatening to shoot down United States U-2 surveillance flights in support of UNSCOM, resulting in a United Nations Security Council Resolution 1137 on November 12, 1997, which imposed the travel ban on Iraqi officials and threatened unspecified "further measures";

Whereas on November 13, 1997, Iraq expelled United States inspectors from Iraq, leading to UNSCOM's decision to pull out its remaining inspectors and resulting in a United Nations Security Council Presidential Statement demanding Iraq revoke the expulsion;

Whereas on January 16, 1998, an UNSCOM team led by American Scott Ritter was withdrawn from Iraq after being barred for three days by Iraq from conducting inspections, resulting in the adoptionof a United Nations Security Council Presidential Statement deploring Iraq's decision to bar the team as a clear violation of all applicable resolutions;

Whereas <<NOTE: Saddam Hussein. Kofi Annan.>> despite clear agreement on the part of Iraqi President Saddam Hussein with United

Nations General Kofi Annan to grant access to all sites, and fully cooperate with UNSCOM, and the adoption on March 2, 1998, of United Nations Security Council Resolution 1154, warning that any violation of the agreement with Annan would have the "severest consequences" for Iraq, Iraq has continued to actively conceal weapons and weapons programs, provide misinformation and otherwise deny UNSCOM inspectors access;

Whereas <<NOTE: Richard Butler.>> on June 24, 1998, UNSCOM Director Richard Butler presented information to the United Nations Security Council indicating clearly that Iraq, in direct contradiction to information provided to UNSCOM, weaponized the nerve agent VX; and

Whereas Iraq's continuing weapons of mass destruction programs threaten vital United States interests and international peace and security:

Now, therefore, be it

[[Page 112 STAT. 1541]]

Resolved by the Senate and House of Representatives of the United States of America in Congress assembled, That the Government of Iraq is in material and unacceptable breach of its international obligations, and therefore the President is urged to take appropriate action, in accordance with the Constitution and relevant laws of the United States, to bring Iraq into compliance with its international obligations.

Approved August 14, 1998.

LEGISLATIVE HISTORY—S.J. Res. 54:

CONGRESSIONAL RECORD, Vol. 144 (1998):
  July 31, considered and passed Senate.
  Aug. 3, considered and passed House.

Appendix V - Iraq Resolution (P.L. 107-243)

PUBLIC LAW 107–243—OCT. 16, 2002
AUTHORIZATION FOR USE OF MILITARY
FORCE AGAINST IRAQ RESOLUTION OF 2002
116 STAT. 1498 PUBLIC LAW 107–243—OCT. 16, 2002
Public Law 107–243
107th Congress
Joint Resolution

To authorize the use of United States Armed Forces against Iraq.

Whereas in 1990 in response to Iraq's war of aggression againstand illegal occupation of Kuwait, the United States forged a coalition of nations to liberate Kuwait and its people in order to defend the national security of the United States and enforce United Nations Security Council resolutions relating to Iraq;

Whereas after the liberation of Kuwait in 1991, Iraq entered into a United Nations sponsored cease-fire agreement pursuant to which Iraq unequivocally agreed, among other things, to eliminate its nuclear, biological, and chemical weapons programs and the means to deliver and develop them, and to end its support for international terrorism;

Whereas the efforts of international weapons inspectors, United States intelligence agencies, and Iraqi defectors led to the discovery that Iraq had large stockpiles of chemical weapons and a large scale biological weapons program, and that Iraq had an advanced nuclear weapons development program that was much closer to producing a nuclear weapon than intelligence reporting had previously indicated;

Whereas Iraq, in direct and flagrant violation of the cease-fire, attempted to thwart the efforts of weapons inspectors to identify and destroy Iraq's weapons of mass destruction stockpiles and development capabilities, which finally resulted in the withdrawal of inspectors from Iraq on October 31, 1998;

Whereas in Public Law 105–235 (August 14, 1998), Congress concluded that Iraq's continuing weapons of mass destruction programs threatened vital United States interests and international peace and security, declared Iraq to be in "material and unacceptable breach of its international obligations" and urged the President "to take appropriate action, in accordance with the Constitution and relevant laws of the United States, to bring Iraq into compliance with its international obligations";

Whereas Iraq both poses a continuing threat to the national security of the United States and international peace and security in the Persian Gulf region and remains in material and unacceptable breach of its international obligations by, among other things, continuing to possess and develop a significant chemical and biological weapons capability, actively seeking a nuclear weapons capability, and supporting and harboring terrorist organizations;

Whereas Iraq persists in violating resolution of the United Nations Security Council by continuing to engage in brutal repression of its civilian population thereby threatening international peace Oct. 16, 2002 and security in the region, by refusing to release, repatriate, or account for non-Iraqi citizens wrongfully detained by Iraq, including an American serviceman, and by failing to return property wrongfully seized by Iraq from Kuwait;

Whereas the current Iraqi regime has demonstrated its capability and willingness to use weapons of mass destruction against other nations and its own people;

Whereas the current Iraqi regime has demonstrated its continuing hostility toward, and willingness to attack, the United States, including by attempting in 1993 to assassinate former President Bush and by firing on many thousands of occasions on United States and Coalition Armed Forces engaged in enforcing the resolutions of the United Nations Security Council;

Whereas members of al Qaida, an organization bearing responsibility for attacks on the United States, its citizens, and interests, including the attacks that occurred on September 11, 2001, are known to be in Iraq;

Whereas Iraq continues to aid and harbor other international terrorist organizations, including organizations that threaten the lives and safety of United States citizens;

Whereas the attacks on the United States of September 11, 2001, underscored the gravity of the threat posed by the acquisition of weapons of mass destruction by international terrorist organizations;

Whereas Iraq's demonstrated capability and willingness to use weapons of mass destruction, the risk that the current Iraqi regime will either employ those weapons to launch a surprise attack against the United States or its Armed Forces or provide them to international terrorists who would do so, and the extreme magnitude of harm that would result to the United States and its citizens from such an attack, combine to justify action by the United States to defend itself;

Whereas United Nations Security Council Resolution 678 (1990) authorizes the use of all necessary means to enforce United Nations Security Council Resolution 660 (1990) and subsequent relevant resolutions and to compel Iraq to cease certain activities that threaten international peace and security, including the development of weapons of mass destruction and refusal or obstruction of United Nations weapons inspections in violation of United Nations Security Council Resolution 687 (1991), repression of its civilian population in violation of United Nations Security Council Resolution 688 (1991), and threatening its neighbors or United Nations operations in Iraq in violation of United Nations Security Council Resolution 949 (1994);

Whereas in the Authorization for Use of Military Force Against Iraq Resolution (Public Law 102–1), Congress has authorized the President "to use United States Armed Forces pursuant to United Nations Security Council Resolution 678 (1990) in order to achieve implementation of Security Council Resolution 660, 661, 662, 664, 665, 666, 667, 669, 670, 674, and 677";

Whereas in December 1991, Congress expressed its sense that it "supports the use of all necessary means to achieve the goals of United Nations Security Council Resolution 687 as being consistent with the Authorization of Use of Military Force Against Iraq Resolution (Public Law 102–1)," that Iraq's repression of its civilian population violates United Nations Security Council Resolution 688 and "constitutes a continuing threat to the peace, security, and stability of the Persian Gulf region," and that Congress, "supports the use of all necessary means to achieve the goals of United Nations Security Council Resolution 688";

Whereas the Iraq Liberation Act of 1998 (Public Law 105–338) expressed the sense of Congress that it should be the policy of the United States to support efforts to remove from power the current Iraqi regime and promote the emergence of a democratic government to replace that regime;

Whereas on September 12, 2002, President Bush committed the United States to "work with the United Nations Security Council to meet our common challenge" posed by Iraq and to "work for the necessary resolutions," while also making clear that "the Security Council resolutions will be enforced, and the just demands of peace and security will be met, or action will be unavoidable";

Whereas the United States is determined to prosecute the war on terrorism and Iraq's ongoing support for international terrorist groups combined with its development of weapons of mass destruction in direct violation of its obligations under the 1991 cease-fire and other United Nations Security Council resolutions make clear that it is in the national security interests of the United States and in furtherance of the war on terrorism that all relevant United Nations Security Council resolutions be enforced, including through the use of force if necessary;

Whereas Congress has taken steps to pursue vigorously the war on terrorism through the provision of authorities and funding requested by the President to take the necessary actions against international terrorists and terrorist organizations, including those nations, organizations, or persons who planned, authorized, committed, or aided the terrorist attacks that occurred on September 11, 2001, or harbored such persons or organizations;

Whereas the President and Congress are determined to continue to take all appropriate actions against international terrorists and terrorist organizations, including those nations, organizations, or persons who planned, authorized, committed, or aided the terrorist attacks that occurred on September 11, 2001, or harbored such persons or organizations;

Whereas the President has authority under the Constitution to take action in order to deter and prevent acts of international terrorism against the United States, as Congress recognized in the joint resolution on Authorization for Use of Military Force (Public Law 107–40); and

Whereas it is in the national security interests of the United States to restore international peace and security to the Persian Gulf region: Now, therefore, be it

Resolved by the Senate and House of Representatives of the United States of America in Congress assembled,

SECTION 1. SHORT TITLE.

This joint resolution may be cited as the "Authorization for Use of Military Force Against Iraq Resolution of 2002". Authorization for Use of Military Force Against Iraq Resolution of 2002. 50 USC 1541 note.

SEC. 2. SUPPORT FOR UNITED STATES DIPLOMATIC EFFORTS.

The Congress of the United States supports the efforts by the President to—

(1) strictly enforce through the United Nations Security Council all relevant Security Council resolutions regarding Iraq and encourages him in those efforts; and

(2) obtain prompt and decisive action by the Security Council to ensure that Iraq abandons its strategy of delay, evasion and noncompliance and promptly and strictly complies with all relevant Security Council resolutions regarding Iraq.

SEC. 3. AUTHORIZATION FOR USE OF UNITED STATES ARMED FORCES.

(a) AUTHORIZATION.—The President is authorized to use the Armed Forces of the United States as he determines to be necessary and appropriate in order to—

(1) defend the national security of the United States against the continuing threat posed by Iraq; and

(2) enforce all relevant United Nations Security Council resolutions regarding Iraq.

(b) PRESIDENTIAL DETERMINATION.—In connection with the exercise of the authority granted in subsection (a) to use force the President shall, prior to such exercise or as soon thereafter as may be feasible, but no later than 48 hours after exercising such authority, make available to the Speaker of the House of Representatives and the President pro tempore of the Senate his determination that—

(1) reliance by the United States on further diplomatic or other peaceful means alone either (A) will not adequately protect the national security of the United States against the continuing threat posed by Iraq or (B) is not likely to lead to enforcement of all relevant United Nations Security Council resolutions regarding Iraq; and

(2) acting pursuant to this joint resolution is consistent with the United States and other countries continuing to take the necessary actions against international terrorist and terrorist organizations, including those nations, organizations, or persons who planned, authorized, committed or aided the terrorist attacks that occurred on September 11, 2001.

(c) WAR POWERS RESOLUTION REQUIREMENTS.—

(1) SPECIFIC STATUTORY AUTHORIZATION.—Consistent with section 8(a)(1) of the War Powers Resolution, the Congress declares that this section is intended to constitute specific statutory authorization within the meaning of section 5(b) of the War Powers Resolution.

(2) APPLICABILITY OF OTHER REQUIREMENTS.—Nothing in this joint resolution supersedes any requirement of the War Powers Resolution.

SEC. 4. REPORTS TO CONGRESS.

(a) REPORTS.—The President shall, at least once every 60 days, submit to the Congress a report on matters relevant to this joint resolution, including actions taken pursuant to the exercise of authority granted in section 3 and the status of planning for efforts that are expected to be required after such actions are completed, including those actions described in section 7 of the Iraq Liberation Act of 1998 (Public Law 105–338).

(b) SINGLE CONSOLIDATED REPORT.—To the extent that the submission of any report described in subsection (a) coincides with the submission of any other report on matters relevant to this joint resolution otherwise required to be submitted to Congress pursuant to the reporting requirements of the War Powers Resolution (Public Law 93–148), all such reports may be submitted as a single consolidated report to the Congress.

14. RULE OF CONSTRUCTION.—To the extent that the information required by section 3 of the Authorization for Use of Military Force Against Iraq Resolution (Public Law 102–1) is included in the report required by this section, such report shall be considered as meeting the requirements of section 3 of such resolution. Approved October 16, 2002.